Death of Democratic Freedoms: A Tangled Web of Trump Loyalists

A guide to the masters, manipulators, and minions of Trump's 2025 presidency

Lesley Gregory

First Edition: 2025

For rights and permissions, please contact:

L Gregory

theimpactnarrative@gmail.com

Text copyright © 2025 Lesley Gregory.

All rights reserved. No portion of this book may be reproduced in any form without permission from the publisher, except as permitted by U.S. copyright law.

Every effort has been made by the author and publishing house to ensure that the information contained in this book was correct as of press time. The author and publishing house hereby disclaim and do not assume liability for any injury, loss, damage, or disruption caused by errors or omissions, regardless of whether any errors or omissions result from negligence, accident, or any other cause. Readers are encouraged to verify any information contained in this book prior to taking any action on the information.

A catalogue record for this book is available from the National Library of Australia and the State Library of Western Australia.

Book design by L Gregory

Editor H Reynolds

ISBN – Paperback: 978-1-7640250-2-7

ISBN – eBook: 978-1-7640250-3-4

For my friend, an avid reader, D.D.

It's autumn and I found my voice...

Also, by Lesley Gregory
Death of Democratic Freedoms Series:
Trump's First 45 Days

"Oh, what a tangled web we weave when first we practice to deceive…"

Sir Walter Scott, Marmion: A Tale of Flodden Field, 1808.

Table of Contents

Dramatis Personae 9

Structure of the Federal Government 12

President 17

Vice President.. 25

Speaker of the House 34

EXECUTIVE DEPARTMENT HEADS 44

Secretary of State 45

Secretary of the Treasury 56

Secretary of Defense 65

Attorney General 77

Secretary of the Interior 88

Secretary of Agriculture.. 94

Secretary of Commerce.. 101

Secretary of Health and Human Services 117

Secretary of Transportation 131

Secretary of Energy 137

Secretary of Veterans Affairs 149

Secretary of Homeland Security 154

MISC. OTHER KEY CABINET POSITIONS................................... 161

Director of National Intelligence.. 162

Chief of Staff 177

Director of the Office of Management and Budget 184

Administrator of the Environmental Protection Agency 190

Administrator of the Small Business Administration 196

U.S. Trade Representative 202

MISC. NON-CABINET ROLES 207

White House Press Secretary 208

Border Czar 213

National Security Adviser 219

Director of the Federal Bureau of Intelligence 225

Tangled Webs 232

Bibliography 239

Master

Master – one having control, especially of a servant, a person who holds another person in subjugation or serfdom.

Manipulator

Manipulator – a person who uses deceptive or underhanded tactics to control or influence others, for their own personal gain, often at the expense of others.

Minion

Minion – a follower, or underling who has little importance and must do what a person at a higher rank orders them to. Replaceable and expendable.

Dramatis Personae

Dramatis Personae, a Latin term for "persons of the drama," refers to the actors in a play and the characters they portray. When metaphorically applied the political arena, these actors often step into roles that blur the line between public persona and private self. The crafting of a public identity becomes an artful deception, an intricate dance in which authenticity is masked by a carefully constructed image.

Politicians, more than most, are masters of this performance, curating their public selves to meet societal expectations and gain influence. Was it truly surprising when disillusioned U.S. voters, frustrated by the inequities of a prestige-driven system, chose a candidate whose persona radiated status and power and who solemnly promised to address their grievances? After all, status is a commanding weapon: wielded by the powerful and coveted by many, driven by desires for validation, legacy, and control over perception. This second book in the *Death of Democratic Freedoms* series is once again offered as a clear and accessible guide; written in straightforward language to assist the person in the street, like the author, in navigating the complexities of key figures in the U.S. political system. It explores the qualifications, connections, and motivations behind Trump's selections for roles such as Vice President, Speaker of the House, and other influential positions. His department heads and a selection of other noteworthy staff appointments are considered, with a focus on their public images; those carefully curated, media-friendly facades designed to enhance their appeal and suggest competence. Their political histories, current personas, and relevant skills are examined to assess their capacity to succeed in the roles they've been given.

To offer broader context, the book also outlines the structure and dynamics between key branches of government, illustrating how each figure fits into the larger political landscape. A concise summary of President Trump's personal and business history is included to provide insight into who he is today and some potential motivations behind his staffing decisions.

If anything became clear during the early months of Trump's second presidential term, it was that his pursuit of power centred on asserting dominance, securing loyalty in critical agencies, and entrenching his position—rather than pursuing meaningful reform or national unity.

But the most pressing questions remained: Why did Trump nominate and install the individuals he did? Was it their steadfast loyalty to his ideology, repayment of political favours, complementary skill sets, or something else entirely? By analysing these central players, I hope to offer readers insight into Trump's motivations and the Dramatis Personae who support, and in some cases are enabling, an "unscheduled catastrophic disassembly" of American democracy.

Because only by asking the right questions can we begin to understand the characters and motives behind America's escalating political crisis.
Asking the wrong question will always yield the wrong answer.

Structure of the Federal Government

Constitutional Division of Power

For over two centuries, the U.S. Constitution has endured as a bedrock of governance, a meticulous blueprint forged to prevent tyranny and safeguard freedom. Its architects, haunted by the spectre of absolute power, constructed a system designed to balance authority with the protection of individual liberties. The framework they devised aimed to secure a delicate equilibrium, one that respects both majority rule and minority rights, defends liberty and equality, and maintains a functional tension between federal and state power.

Central to this design is the doctrine of Separation of Powers, a deliberate division of authority among three branches of government: the legislative branch, embodied by Congress; the executive branch, led by the President; and the judicial branch, presided over by the Supreme Court. This structure was not merely an exercise in governance but an act of defiance against the consolidation of power. Its purpose was clear: to ensure that no single entity could ever seize control and bend the nation to its will.

The Constitution's very essence lies in its struggle to contain power. The Founders understood that the true danger lay not only in the hands of a tyrannical monarch but also in the creeping corruption of elites or the unpredictable whims of an authoritarian president. To safeguard against these threats, power was split not just horizontally between the three branches of government but vertically between the national government and the states in a system known as federalism. This dual framework aimed to establish a government that serves the common good by promoting deliberation, curbing abuses, and encouraging compromise.

Yet this intricate mechanism was only as strong as its weakest link. The Founders constructed a system of checks and balances, an elaborate interplay of authority designed to prevent any one branch from overpowering the others. Congress was granted the power to shape the executive and judicial branches, raise revenue, declare war, and craft laws essential to carrying out its duties. While the President could veto legislative acts, Congress could override those vetoes with a two-thirds majority in both houses. Additionally, the Senate held the authority to review and approve critical executive and judicial appointments and to ratify treaties.

This intricate design, grounded in the principles of separation of powers, checks and balances, and federalism, became the cornerstone of American governance. But that cornerstone has been tested repeatedly, its resilience strained under the relentless pressure of political manoeuvring and executive overreach. Since Trump's 2025 inauguration, it is prudent to consider whether a system designed to resist tyranny can withstand a leader intent on bending its principles to his will.

Branches of Government

The American experiment rests upon three distinct branches of government, each with its own powers, limitations, and responsibilities. However, if these divisions begin to blur and loyalty to a single figure takes hold it could destabilise the entire structure.

The legislative branch, composed of the House of Representatives and the Senate (Congress), has long been considered the voice of the people. It holds the authority to draft and pass laws, confirm or reject presidential nominations for federal agencies, federal judges, and the Supreme Court, and even declare war. Yet its power is only as effective as its willingness to act. A complacent or complicit Congress becomes nothing more than an instrument of the executive's will.

The executive branch, driven by the President, Vice President, and the Cabinet, wields the power of enforcement and administration. The President, as both head of state and Commander in Chief of the armed forces, commands vast authority. The Vice President serves primarily as a presidential support figure, stepping in when the President is unable to fulfil the role and casting tie-breaking votes in the Senate. Meanwhile, the Cabinet, composed of department heads and high-ranking officials nominated by the President and approved by the Senate, serves as the chief advisory body. But when those entrusted with power answer to a leader whose motivations are suspect, we must consider the validity of their counsel.

The judicial branch, including the Supreme Court and lower federal courts, holds the solemn duty of interpreting the law, applying it to individual cases, and determining whether legislation and executive actions violate the Constitution. Yet even the judiciary is not immune to political influence. When appointments are made with partisan interests at heart, and these interests are brought into play, the maintenance of the court's impartiality may be sorely tested.

These branches were designed to function in harmony, but when one begins to tip the balance, the entire system quakes.

Checks and Balances
The system of checks and balances was crafted as a defence against overreach, a safeguard intended to halt the accumulation of power within any single branch. But like all safeguards, its strength is only as great as the integrity of those who wield it.

The legislative branch, entrusted with creating the laws of the land, must contend with a President who holds the power of the veto. While Congress can override this veto with a supermajority, the power struggle is never truly settled. At any moment, the judicial branch can intervene, declaring legislation unconstitutional and thereby nullifying the will of both Congress and the President.

Yet the legislative branch retains formidable weapons of its own. It controls the purse strings of government, approves presidential nominations, and even possesses the ultimate authority to impeach and remove the President from office. Assuming those powers have not been weakened by political calculation, partisan loyalty, or sheer intimidation.

The executive branch, charged with enforcing the law, can attempt to circumvent the legislative process through executive orders. But this power is not absolute. The courts can strike down those orders if they overstep constitutional boundaries.

The judicial branch serves as the final arbiter of constitutional interpretation. But its authority and objectivity can hang on the independence of its appointments. The President nominates judges, the Senate confirms them, and Congress holds the power to impeach and remove those deemed unfit. If these appointments are driven by political loyalty rather than judicial competence, the very notion of impartial justice is thrown into question.

This delicate interplay of power was meant to be a sturdy buffer against despotism. But if one branch refuses to fulfill its role the very safeguards intended to protect democracy have the capacity to become instruments of its destruction.

President

Donald John Trump – June 14, 1946

Estimated net worth, January 2025 - $6.7 Billion

Trump appears acutely attentive that he is perpetually performing, navigating life as if constantly aware of being watched. While all people are inherently social actors, Trump seems to embody this trait to an extraordinary degree.

The Early Years

Donald Trump was born in New York and is the fourth of five children of Mary Anne MacLeod Trump and her husband New York real estate tycoon Frederick Christ Trump Sr. During his early years Trump's mother was unwell and often hospitalised, leaving his father as the main influence on the children. But his father's parental skills or lack thereof were akin to parental bullying, leading to no emotional attachment or encouragement for the children, incessant criticism and what we now understand to be toxic positivity.

His father's behaviour affected Trump for life, manifesting in narcissistic behaviour, bullying, and self-importance that first played out in his early years. At the age of 13, he was sent to the New York Military Academy by his father to deal with his "behavioural difficulties" and to instil a sense of discipline. His mother, not knowing how to discipline him, is believed to have been relieved by this decision.

Trump's aggressive behaviour, encouraged by his father, would lead to his lifelong belief that acting as the "tough guy" was the way to success. His father frequently pitted him against his older brother Freddy, praising Trump's bold, assertive behaviour and positioning him as the "heir apparent" when Freddy chose to become a pilot; a choice their father viewed as a failure. Tragically, Freddy died at 42 from alcoholism, a sad outcome considering his troubled upbringing. However, his death had a lasting impact on Trump, leading him to avoid alcohol and cigarettes throughout his life.

Trump's business career began while he was still attending the Wharton School at the University of Pennsylvania, making investments in Philadelphia real estate. After completing his studies, he returned to New York to join the family business full-time.

Women in Trump's Life

Trump's first wife, Ivana Zelnickova, was a Czech athlete and model. They had three children together Donald Jr., Ivanka, and Eric before finally divorcing in 1990. Their bitter divorce proceedings prompted headlines in gossip columns, with Ivana alleging acts of domestic abuse, which she later tempered.

He later married actress Marla Maples in 1993, just two months after their only child, Tiffany, was born. The couple divorced in 1999, and Trump went on to marry his current wife Melania Knauss in 2005, a former model from Slovenia. They have a son, Barron William Trump.

Trump, as a politician, has had unrelenting allegations of sexual misconduct and extramarital affairs brought against him. One of the most infamous cases involved 34 felony counts of falsifying business records to cover up a hush money arrangement, with adult-film actress Stormy Daniels, over an alleged 2006 extramarital affair. Trump was convicted on all 34 charges.

The Business of Making Money

Under Trump's watch, the family business pivoted from his father's residential units in Brooklyn and Queens to upscale grand Manhattan projects. Possibly Trump's most renowned property and his home for many years, Trump Tower, was constructed on Fifth Avenue, New York, in 2001. Over the years, many properties carrying the Trump name were developed, ranging from casinos and condominiums to golf courses and hotels, spanning various locations worldwide, including Atlantic City, Chicago, and Las Vegas, as well as India, Türkiye, and the Philippines.

Trump then branched out into the entertainment world through ownership of the Miss Universe, Miss USA, and Miss Teen USA beauty pageants. But what introduced him to the masses and made him a household name was the *NBC* reality show, The Apprentice, that ran for 14 seasons. He has also written several books, made cameo appearances in movies, and sold a myriad of products from drinks to ties.

However, even with the benefit of family money and his father's business guidance, Trump has filed business bankruptcies on six occasions, with several of his ventures including Trump Steak's and Trump University collapsing. He has actively refused to reveal any taxation information, even though this is the norm for U.S. presidents. However, a *New York Times* 2020 investigation revealed years of financial losses and income tax avoidance.

Presidential Aspirations

Trump briefly considered running for president with the Reform Party in 2000 and again as a Republican in 2012. However, it wasn't until June 2015 that he officially launched his presidential campaign, proclaiming the American Dream dead but vowing to revive it on a larger and grander scale.

During his unconventional presidential launch speech, Trump bragged about his wealth and business achievements, accused Mexico of sending drugs, criminals, and rapists to the U.S., and vowed to make Mexico pay for a border wall. His dominating presence during debates and his controversy-laden policy platform drew both passionate supporters and harsh critics, along with an overwhelming amount of media attention, especially from right-wing media outlets.

From the very beginning of his first term, Trump introduced unprecedented drama to the presidency, making official announcements via social media and openly confronting foreign leaders. This drama would follow him through the interim years between his presidential terms and into his second term as president in 2025.

Will the Real Donald Trump Please Stand Up?

Possibly Trump's single greatest achievement in life was building the brand of Donald J. Trump, Self-Made Billionaire. So effective has this brand been, it generated hundreds of millions of dollars through television shows, books, merchandising, and licensing deals. Is it possible that Trump's brand has become so deeply entrenched that the "real" Donald Trump — or the person he might have been — has been lost to time, beyond even his own ability to reclaim it?

Building that brand took more than just his father's wealth. Equally crucial were Trump's marketing savvy and relentless, deal-making drive. While his father provided the financial backing for the trappings of wealth, Trump transformed them into a captivating story. His father's money was instrumental in constructing Trump Tower, the symbol of privilege that established Trump as a key figure in New York. However, he was the one who understood and capitalised on Trump Tower's iconic status, using it as a central stage for both the reality TV show, The Apprentice, and his presidential campaign.

Throughout his life, Trump has earned a widespread reputation as an exceptionally disagreeable person. Individuals with this trait are often callous, rude, arrogant, and lacking empathy. If Trump doesn't rank low on agreeableness, likely no one does.

Over-the-top extroversion combined with elevated levels of disagreeableness are not traits expected of a U.S. president. A key characteristic of high extroversion is an unending drive to seek rewards. Highly extroverted individuals are motivated to chase positive emotional experiences whether through social approval, fame, or wealth. For extroverts, the joy lies more in the pursuit of their goals than in achieving them.

Trump's drive for social dominance and aggressiveness was apparent from a young age, with the core of his personality appearing to be fuelled by anger. Trump's anger is a dominant emotion that seems to feed both his extroversion and his disagreeable nature. While his anger has inspired hostility, it also drives his quest for social dominance and his desire to earn admiration. Paired with a sharp, often aggressive sense of humour, anger forms the essence of Trump's charisma and is evident in his political rhetoric.

Although Trump's personal life reflects aspects of his public persona, such as assertiveness and a relentless work ethic, certain traits such as his avoidance of drugs and alcohol and his minimal need for sleep, may provide deeper insight into his private character.

By the age of three family annual distributions from his father's business empire, of what would be equivalent to $200,000 in today's money, made him a millionaire by the age of eight. At 17, he held part ownership of a 52-unit apartment building gifted by his father. Shortly after finishing college, he was receiving around $1 million per year from his father; a sum that grew over time to more than $5 million annually throughout his 40s and 50s.

There's no denying that Trump's privilege played a pivotal role in shaping the person he is today, but at what price? His public and private selves have become so blurred; tangled in an exhausting loop of seeking validation and winning at all costs. The desperate need to earn his father's approval and prove his worth has forged a man who appears forever haunted by the unhealed wounds of his youth, endlessly chasing something that remains just out of reach.

When Trump faces adversity, it's as if he retreats to a childlike state, lashing out with insults or personal attacks, throwing verbal tantrums to shut down conversations. If not that, he shifts focus to something he claims to have done well, desperately trying to redirect praise his way, much like a child craving approval. He seems more willing to twist the truth or make misleading statements than admit defeat, clinging to the same irrational tactics children often use when backed into a corner.

Privilege was also the enabler of his flawed character; for without privilege he could never have accumulated the power and following that he has. His wealth and family connections paved the way for his meteoric rise in a corrupt and greedy system that rewards the entitled and punishes the already downtrodden. In a world that venerates wealth, fame, and elitism, Trump became the poster boy for success built on the suffering of the American working class. Ironically, the white working-class segment of U.S. society now encompasses the majority of his voter base.

With President Donald Trump, what you see is genuinely what you get. He follows through on his words with unshakable confidence, paying little attention to the consequences and showing scant empathy, firmly believing that his viewpoint is the correct one. Yet, there lies a fatal flaw, an unwillingness to shoulder responsibility. Trump refuses to accept blame for any missteps, always shifting the fault onto others. But how long can this deflection continue before it catches up with him?

After interviewing Trump in the 1990s, Mark Singer of *The New Yorker* left the meeting with the impression that Trump had achieved *"an existence unmolested by the rumblings of a soul."*

Vice President

James David Vance – August 2, 1984

Estimated net worth, March 2025 - $10 Million

There is an elemental variability surrounding Vice President J.D. Vance, clear in his willingness to change his stance and principles according to the vagaries of the political moment. The man appears able to be whomever you'd like him to be.

The Early Years

Vance, whose birth name was James Donald Bowman, was born in Middletown, Ohio, to Donald Bowman and Beverly Bowman (née Vance). His biological parents divorced when he was a toddler, with his mother going on to marry Bob Hamel. Hamel formally adopted Vance, whereupon his mother changed his name to James David Hamel, removing his biological father's name, Donald, but preserving his nickname, JD.

His mother and her second husband eventually divorced. Vance later moved in with his maternal grandparents, who raised him, as his mother struggled with drug addiction and her behaviour became increasingly erratic. In April 2013, he became James David Vance after taking his grandmother's surname.

Following his high school graduation in 2003, he joined the Marine Corps and served as a corporal in Iraq with the Public Affairs division of the 2nd Marine Aircraft Wing. He later earned a degree in political science and philosophy from Ohio State University before enrolling at Yale Law School in 2010. During his time at Yale, he met Usha Chilukuri, who would become his wife and the mother of their three children. The couple married in 2014 and also had a traditional ceremony where a Hindu pundit blessed them.

Vance's 2016 memoir, *Hillbilly Elegy*, became a bestseller, catapulting him into the public spotlight. The book argued that the downfall of post-industrial America was primarily driven by social issues within the white working class, rather than the commonly acknowledged collapse of the U.S. industrial economy.

Vance argued that the lack of agency and control in the lives of white working-class people, along with their willingness to blame others for their problems, was a key factor in this decline. Possibly a little prophetically, a *New York Times* review described the book as *"... insightful sociological analysis of the white underclass that has fuelled the politics of rebellion, especially the rise of Donald J. Trump."*

By 2020, Vance's perspective on the decline of post-industrial America had notably shifted; he now attributed the blame, not to white working-class Americans, but to tax cuts for the wealthy, the decline of the traditional American family, and China's increasing influence on American imports, which resulted in widespread U.S. job losses.

Political Ascension

After graduating from Yale in 2013, Vance served as a clerk for a federal judge in Kentucky and briefly worked in corporate law. He quickly left the legal profession and relocated to San Francisco to join Mithril Capital, a firm founded by billionaire Peter Thiel. He then became a partner at venture capital fund, Rise of the Rest. Eventually, Vance returned to southwest Ohio, settling in an affluent Cincinnati neighbourhood, where he launched his own venture fund, Narya Capital. The fund's investments include a farmland investment platform, a Catholic prayer and meditation app (Vance converted to Catholicism in 2019), and a right-leaning video platform.

During the 2016 U.S. presidential election, Vance strongly opposed Trump, identifying as a *"Never Trump"* advocate. He criticised Trump as *"cultural heroin,"* harmful, and accused him of steering the white working class toward a dark future. He wavered between viewing Trump as a cynical figure similar to former President Nixon or as a dangerous figure, whom he described as *"America's Hitler."*

Nevertheless, during Trump's first term, Vance's political perspective changed. He increasingly supported Trump's policies and became aggravated by what he perceived as an exaggerated liberal backlash. Vance saw that even acknowledging Trump's reasonable points provoked extreme reactions. He now positioned himself as a conservative advocate for the overlooked and marginalised; shifting his focus away from criticising the people he grew up with to critiquing the professional class he had risen into.

By 2020, Vance voted for Trump.

Vance launched his Senate campaign in Ohio in 2021, and while campaigning, referred to his previous remarks about Trump: *"I regret being wrong about the guy,"* later calling him, *"the best president of my lifetime."* From labelling Trump *"America's Hitler"* to calling him *"the best president of my lifetime"* is quite a dramatic shift. By April 2022, Trump had endorsed Vance, and in typical Trump style, announced, *"JD is kissing my ass — he wants my support so bad."* Vance ultimately won the Ohio Senate seat with a 53% to 47% victory.

Vance is a prominent critic of U.S. support for Ukraine, stating in a 2022 interview with Steve Bannon* of the alt-right *War Room* podcast, *"I've got to be honest — I don't really care what happens to Ukraine either way."* He has also expressed that had he been in former Vice President Mike Pence's position in 2021, he would not have certified the 2020 election results; a stance many Americans strongly oppose. Additionally, he has urged Trump to ignore the Supreme Court if the justices block him from firing executive branch officials.

*(*Steve Bannon was Trump's campaign chairman and chief strategist for seven months in 2017.)*

Political Ascension: Helpful Connections

Vance's main allies within Trump's inner circle were Donald Trump Jr. and Eric Trump. His strongest backing in conservative media came from Tucker Carlson, and his largest financial supporter was Peter Thiel, who donated $10 million to his Senate campaign.

While at Yale, Vance attended a lecture by Peter Thiel — the billionaire tech investor and author of *The Education of a Libertarian,* an essay thought to have influenced the *Mandate for Leadership* document of Project 2025. Vance is said to have referred to Thiel's talk as the most significant moment of his time at Yale; even more impactful than the moment he met his future wife, Usha Chilukuri.

The connection to Thiel was solidified when Thiel arranged Vance's first meeting with Trump. Thiel, who had previously supported Vance's venture capital firm, had in recent years become a key figure helping MAGA-aligned Republicans like Vance. Thiel then travelled to Palm Beach to personally ensure that the introduction between Vance and Trump went smoothly.

After the meeting in Palm Beach, Vance was invited by a friend to play golf at Trump's golf club, where Trump typically spent his winters and springs, playing and dining daily. On the day of his invitation, after the round of golf, Vance walked into the clubhouse where Trump was having lunch. As Vance entered, a patron asked if he was the author of *Hillbilly Elegy* and requested his autograph. Vance then shook hands and took photos with other club members. Trump, who had been observing Vance, is said to have turned to Chris Ruddy, CEO of *Newsmax* and longtime Mar-a-Lago member, and remarked, *"Do you know the great J.D. Vance? I hope Newsmax is helping him."*

In an effort to secure Trump's support, Vance reached out to ally and former *Fox News* anchor Tucker Carlson, requesting he vouch for him. While Trump and Carlson weren't in regular contact after Trump's first term, Carlson still had enough influence to catch Trump's attention. A further contributing factor in Trump's final decision to support Vance was Vance's friendship with his sons Donald Trump Jr. and Eric Trump, who had been some of Vance's most steadfast supporters.

Sidekick or Stooge?

The only formal criteria for a vice president are that they be a natural-born U.S. citizen, at least 35 years old, and a resident of the U.S. for at least 14 years prior to holding the position.

The main duties of the vice president include taking over as president if the sitting president dies, becomes disabled, or is impeached; assuming the role of President of the Senate; and casting a deciding vote if Congress is deadlocked. Informally, the vice president also represents the president at public events, performs ceremonial duties, acts as a presidential adviser, and meets with heads of state or government. To successfully fulfil his role, Vance needs three things: access to the president and the policy process, Trump's willingness to seek or accept his aid, and the capacity to carry out these roles effectively.

Trump is extremely sensitive to any form of criticism, and due to Vance's unfavourable public image early in the 2025 presidency, Trump had already begun to display a lack of confidence in him. When asked if he would endorse Vance as his successor, Trump responded with a firm "No," this was within the first month of Vance's vice presidency. Given this, it seems clear that Trump is unlikely to take advice from Vance unless it aligns with his own views. Now in his second term, Trump has a loyal group of followers to carry out his wishes and no longer requires a well-connected, experienced vice president, as he did with Mike Pence, to guide his administration.

Vance has few assets to offer Trump in an advisory role. With just two years in the Senate, he lacks the experience traditionally expected of a vice president in managing congressional relations. Additionally, Vance is not well-versed in policy or the workings of government bureaucracy and has no established relationships with key voter groups. As a political novice, he also lacks a strong network of aides and policy experts to support him or populate the administration.

Vance meets the formal criteria and is presumably capable of fulfilling the informal duties. But why did

Trump ultimately choose, out of all available candidates, such an inexperienced politician as his vice president? And how might this play out for the U.S.?

Trump takes pleasure in watching candidates grovel and backtrack to prove their loyalty. Vance had once proudly called himself a *"Never Trump guy."* But by securing backing from billionaire Peter Thiel and fully adopting an America First platform, he succeeded in convincing Trump of his loyalty.

Vance's willingness to abandon his principles in pursuit of power is reflected in his complete reversal from decrying Trump to singing his praises. He shifted blame from the white working class for their social predicaments to Chinese imports and tax cuts for the wealthy. Vance's beard, first seen during the launch of his 2022 Senate campaign, was also a strategic move in his pursuit of power and influence. It symbolised his new political identity, an attempt to project rugged masculinity. He presented himself as a tough, self-reliant outsider who rejected elitist norms, clearly in a bid to appeal to MAGA conservatives. His appearance now strongly resembles that of Donald Trump Jr.

(Chameleon – one who can change appearance at will in order to fit in different environments).

While Trump likely valued Vance's media savvy and ability to appeal to younger working-class Americans, he is also known to be particularly fixated on winning over and ultimately dominating former critics. Vance achieved exactly what he sought by playing the game on Trump's terms.

An inexperienced vice president may not concern Trump, as for much of U.S. history, the role was mostly symbolic. Additionally, Trump is in no rush to think about a successor and has even "jokingly" entertained the notion of serving a third term; despite this currently being Constitutionally restricted.

However, the idea of the vice presidency being merely symbolic was sorely tested in 1945 when President Franklin D. Roosevelt passed away, leaving his successor Harry Truman completely uninformed about the atomic bomb and Roosevelt's postwar strategy.

Eight U.S. presidents have died while in office. Considering Trump's age, unknown health status, and two prior impeachments, the possibility of Vance stepping into the role of president cannot be ignored. With numerous global challenges at hand and the turmoil caused by Trump's second term, the U.S. cannot afford another unprepared or misdirected leader.

Speaker of the House

James Michael Johnson – January 30, 1972

Estimated net worth, March 2025 - $5 Million

Speaker Mike Johnson holds deeply misogynistic and anti-LGBTQ+ views. He has harshly criticised no-fault divorce laws—a feminist victory of the 20th century that granted women the right to end marriages without needing to prove infidelity or abuse. Johnson has argued that women's autonomy in leaving marriages, along with their right to choose motherhood, is to blame for the rise in mass shootings.

His views, that gay people are sinful and inferior, that women should be subjugated to men and restricted from living independently or making choices about their bodies, and that marriage should serve as a means for men to wield absolute control, resonate with a powerful faction within the Republican Party. This toxic ideology has now secured a foothold in the speakership, putting its dangerous influence second in line, behind the vice president, for the U.S. presidency.

This is the true character of Speaker of the House James Michael Johnson, despite his efforts to soften his public rhetoric in order to secure his current position of power.

The Early Years

Johnson was born in Shreveport, Louisiana—the state's third-largest city—and is the oldest of four children to

James Patrick and Jeanne Johnson, who later divorced. His father, a firefighter, was severely burned and disabled in the line of duty in a 1984 cold storage facility fire. Despite doctors' grim prognosis, his father's recovery was seen by 12-year-old Johnson as a miracle, sparking a deepening of his faith.

Johnson earned a Bachelor of Science in business administration and a law degree from Louisiana State University. In 1999, he married Kelly Lary, and together they have four biological children.

In the mid-2010s, Johnson established Freedom Guard, a ministry focused on legal advocacy. He was a "young Earth creationist," a group of Christians who interpret Genesis literally and believe that the Earth is only a few thousand years old and that humans coexisted with dinosaurs. He served as both the attorney and a partner for Kentucky's Creation Museum and Ark Encounter amusement park, which promote "Earth creationist" beliefs as scientific truth.

Missing from Johnson's biography and his congressional website is the fact that he spent two years, from September 2010 through August 2012, as the founding Dean of Louisiana College's Pressler School of Law. The law school spent around $5.5 million in development but never admitted a single student. Louisiana College President Joe Aguillard, who hired Johnson, ended his tenure in controversy due to multiple scandals. Devout Southern Baptist Judge Paul Pressler, the law school's namesake, was later accused of molesting and assaulting teenage boys.

There is absolutely no intention to associate Speaker Johnson with the actions of either Aguillard or Pressler; mentioning Johnson's time as dean is simply part of his overall history.

Political Ascension

Johnson is closely connected to a group of religious leaders who have pushed to diminish or eliminate the separation of church and state, advocating for stronger Christian influence in U.S. governance. Many within this group support the "Seven Mountains mandate;" a belief that Christians are obligated by God to dominate seven key areas of society, business, education, entertainment, family, government, media, and religion.

Johnson's political agenda is driven entirely by his evangelical Christian beliefs (Southern Baptist). His rapid rise to power in Washington has led some to express concern that these strong religious convictions will shape his political positions on high-profile culture war issues such as abortion and LGBTQ+ rights.

A staunch conservative, Johnson is best known for his unwavering support of Donald Trump's efforts to challenge the 2020 election results. A former constitutional lawyer, he signed an amicus brief, a legal document filed by someone with an interest in a case but not directly involved, in a lawsuit seeking to overturn

Pennsylvania's election outcome, and he publicly encouraged Trump to "keep fighting."

Before entering Congress, Johnson worked as a lawyer focused on religious freedom cases, including successfully defending Louisiana's same-sex marriage ban in 2004. He served as a senior attorney for the "Alliance Defending Freedom" from 2002 to 2010. This organisation was behind the legal strategy in the *303 Creative v. Elenis* lawsuit, which led to a Supreme Court ruling allowing a wedding website designer to refuse service to same-sex couples. It also played a pivotal role in the overturning of *Roe v. Wade* in 2022, which had previously recognised the constitutional right to abortion.

In 2016, Johnson won a seat in the House of Representatives, representing Louisiana's 4th district. He was re-elected in 2018, 2020, and 2022.

In October 2023, after three weeks of chaos during which Republicans ousted their fifth Speaker, Kevin McCarthy, and struggled to unite behind a replacement, Johnson rose from relative obscurity to claim one of Washington's most powerful positions: Speaker of the House.

Before assuming the speakership, Johnson had served as chair of the conservative Republican Study Committee and as vice-chair of the House Republican Conference but had no major leadership experience. As October 2023 drew to a close, he emerged as a compromise candidate in a fractured party. His short tenure in the House and low-profile nature meant he had made few enemies. His firm conservative values and support for Trump's 2020 election denialism satisfied the far-right, while his soft-spoken demeanour made him broadly acceptable to more moderate Republicans.

Johnson is a sceptic of climate science and has received more campaign donations from the oil and gas industry than from any other sector during his time in Congress. Downplaying the significance of climate change; this stance is influenced by his creationist views, which maintain that climate change is part of the planet's natural cycles rather than a crisis caused by human activity.

The 2025 vote to re-elect Johnson as Speaker tested Trump's hold over the Republican Party. Trump had urged lawmakers to support Johnson, who had promised to push an aggressive agenda centred on tax cuts and mass deportations. Johnson's bid only survived after Trump paused a round of golf to personally intervene, convincing two Republican senators to reconsider their choice of candidate. Following their conversation with Trump, the senators changed their votes in Johnson's favour.

Quiet Achiever or Religious Crusader?

The Speaker of the House wields significant power in Washington, overseeing House operations, standing second in line to the presidency after the vice president, and playing a vital role in procedures under the 25th Amendment that address presidential disability. As leader of the House majority party, the Speaker sets the legislative agenda and can vote on matters as the representative of their Congressional district.

In this capacity, the Speaker acts as a central mediator between the House, the president, and the Senate. The role includes initiating and advancing legislation, managing the budget, and exercising "the power of the purse," the constitutional authority to tax and allocate government spending.

During Trump's first term, Johnson transitioned from relative obscurity to become a key member of the president's inner circle. He frequently accompanied Trump on Air Force One to football games, rallies, and Republican primaries. This represented a dramatic shift from his position in 2017, when Johnson, then a freshman congressman, felt rattled and uncertain about his political future following a tense call with Trump. Johnson had voted against Trump's initial push to repeal the *Affordable Care Act* (Obamacare), which led to a scathing rebuke from the president.

Although Republicans had campaigned in 2016 on repealing Obamacare, Johnson and other members of the far-right Freedom Caucus objected to the hastily drafted bill presented in 2017. Believing the legislation was poorly constructed, Johnson refused to support it, contributing to its failure. Trump's displeasure was swift and personal.

However, Johnson's path to redemption began following his re-election in 2018, when House Republicans elected him chairman of the influential Republican Study Committee, a post previously held by figures like former Vice President Mike Pence. This position helped Johnson re-establish himself with Trump, aided by the president's frequent visits to Louisiana and Johnson's increasing public support.

Johnson's standing surged further when he served on the House Judiciary Committee during Trump's first impeachment. He became one of the president's most vocal defenders and was later appointed to Trump's Senate impeachment defence team. Johnson also took a leading role in the effort to overturn the 2020 election results.

In the aftermath of Trump's defeat, Johnson pushed baseless claims about election software having ties to authoritarian regimes, but it was his more strategic argument claiming that changes to voting procedures in some states during the Covid-19 pandemic were unconstitutional that gained traction. Johnson argued that altering voting laws without state legislature approval violated the Constitution. Roughly three-quarters of the 146 Republicans who voted against certifying the election cited this rationale.

In late March 2025, Speaker Johnson suggested that the U.S. federal court system should be defunded, restructured, or potentially eliminated. He pointed to the judiciary's refusal to support Trump's increasingly extreme policies as justification. Although he later claimed his comments were theoretical, during a press conference Johnson told reporters: *"We have power of funding over the courts and all these other things. Desperate times call for desperate measures, and Congress is going to act."*

Trump may have endorsed Johnson not only for his loyalty, but also for his legal intellect and religious zeal. Once criticised by Trump for disloyalty, Johnson ultimately became a legal architect of the president's efforts to consolidate power. But the deeper question remains, was Johnson simply swept up in Trump's cult of personality, or is he leveraging Trump's influence as a vehicle to insert his own religious agenda into American politics?

Johnson's transformation from opposing Trump's healthcare agenda to championing his impeachment defence and leading the push to overturn election results suggests a man with a longer-term strategy. Whether motivated by belief, ambition, or both, Johnson's trajectory reflects a shift towards authoritarian religiosity cloaked in constitutional rhetoric.

Generally, both religious and secular Americans agree that it is dangerous when faith institutions formally endorse political candidates or align with parties. Such moves risk eroding the constitutional barrier between church and state, paving the way for an unofficial state religion and disadvantaging non-believers. There are also concerns that if churches endorse candidates, they could exploit their tax-exempt status under the Internal Revenue Service to fundraise for partisan purposes turning faith communities into powerful political machines.

The Johnson Amendment, passed in 1954 and named after then-Senator Lyndon B. Johnson, sought to preserve this separation. It prohibits religious organisations from directly or indirectly participating in political campaigns. However, Mike Johnson played a leading role in introducing legislation in 2021 aimed at repealing this safeguard. He advocates for church involvement in electoral politics; one would assume as long as it aligns with his interpretation of faith.

Johnson's approach edges toward theocracy, a form of government led by religious authorities, rather than a pluralistic democracy built on diverse representation. His belief in white Christian nationalism, coupled with his legislative power, makes him arguably the most openly theocratic figure ever to serve as Speaker of the House.

Now second in line to the presidency, Mike Johnson stands at a critical crossroads. Whether, going forward, he acts as a quiet achiever or a religious crusader, his actions undoubtedly will help determine whether the

U.S. drifts further toward religious authoritarianism or holds fast to its democratic and secular foundations.

EXECUTIVE DEPARTMENT HEADS

Secretary of State

Marco Antonio Rubio – May 28, 1971

Estimated net worth, March 2025 - $1 Million

Marco Rubio defies the typical image of a social conservative. While he regularly attends church with his wife Jeanette and their four children, he is also a lifelong hip-hop fan, often expressing admiration for cultural icons such as Grandmaster Flash and Tupac Shakur.

Fluent in both English and Spanish, Rubio is a strategic asset to the Republican Party, which has long struggled with declining support among Hispanic voters. A foreign policy enthusiast, he is seen by many as one of the few Republican figures capable of expanding Trump's coalition to include more Hispanic Americans and suburban women.

The Early Years

Rubio's story begins with his parents; Father Mario a bartender and mother Oriales a housemaid: Cuban refugees who fled their homeland in 1956, seeking a better life in the United States. Marco Antonio Rubio was born 15 years later, the second of four children, raised in Miami's tightly-knit Cuban-American neighbourhoods. For five years, the family lived in Las Vegas, where they briefly converted to Mormonism before returning to their Catholic roots.

After Fidel Castro took control of Cuba in 1959, the Rubio family resolved never to return. Although Marco has never visited the island, Cuba remains central to his political identity. For Rubio, the pursuit of the American Dream is deeply personal, his family's journey from exile to opportunity mirrors that of many others who have sought refuge in the U.S.

Rubio attended Henry M. Flagler Elementary and later graduated from South Miami Senior High School in 1989. His family eventually settled in Hialeah; a local neighbourhood so heavily Cuban that Spanish often took precedence over English.

By 1990, Rubio had become an active Republican, earning a summer internship with Representative Ileana Ros-Lehtinen, the first Cuban-American woman elected to Congress. Two years later, he volunteered for Lincoln Diaz-Balart's first congressional campaign, where he met and formed a lasting political bond with Mark Rivera, a rising figure in Florida politics.

After a brief stint on a football scholarship at Tarkio College in Missouri, Rubio completed his undergraduate studies at the University of Florida in 1993, and went on to earn his Juris Doctor, cum laude, from the University of Miami School of Law in 1996. His admission to law school was supported by references from Ros-Lehtinen and Diaz-Balart.

Rubio's legal career began at a firm led by Al Cardenas, a Cuban-born Republican strategist and close ally of the well-known political Bush family. In 1996, Rubio was recruited to work on Bob Dole's presidential campaign and later played a key role in helping longtime friend Mark Rivera win a seat in the Florida House of Representatives in 2002.

In 1998, Rubio married Jeanette Dousdebes-Rubio, a former Miami Dolphins cheerleader who had worked with billionaire philanthropist Norman Braman. They were married at the Church of the Little Flower in Coral Gables, a Catholic parish popular among Miami's affluent Hispanic community. The couple have four children.

Political Ascension

From the outset, Rubio aligned himself with Miami's powerful Cuban exile community. Just two years after earning his law degree, he was elected to the West Miami City Commission. He then served in the Florida House of Representatives from 2000 to 2008, taking on roles as Majority Whip, Majority Leader, and ultimately, Speaker of the House. In 2005, Governor Jeb Bush honoured Rubio with a ceremonial sword, naming him the first Cuban-American Speaker of the Florida House.

In the two years leading up to the speakership, Rubio travelled across Florida hosting "Idearaisers," public forums designed to gather citizen input. The top 100 ideas were compiled into a book, all of which passed the House. Of those, 57 were signed into law covering topics such as combating gang violence, promoting energy efficiency, expanding school choice, and helping small businesses access affordable health insurance.

Rubio's legislative focus also included efforts to build a world-class public school system, emphasising performance accountability and addressing underlying socio-economic disparities. After his tenure as Speaker, Rubio returned to private legal practice, took on a visiting professorship at Florida International University, chaired the Florida chapter of GOPAC*, and served as a political analyst for media outlet *Univision* during the 2008 election cycle.
(*Global Organisation of Parliamentarians Against Corruption)

In 2010, Rubio won a surprise victory in Florida's U.S. Senate race, defeating former Governor Charlie Crist. His campaign was propelled by the Tea Party movement, strong Cuban-American backing, and shrewd political strategy. Notably, Rubio offered quiet support to Democrat Kendrick Meek, knowing it would split the vote and weaken Crist, who was running as an independent.

The Cuban-American political establishment played a central role in Rubio's rise. Unlike many other immigrant groups, Cuban exiles have long held disproportionate influence over Miami and Florida politics. Since the 1960s, they've shaped American foreign policy toward Cuba and wielded electoral power in local, state, and national elections.

Rubio frequently refers to himself as the "son of exiles," portraying his family as victims of Fidel Castro's regime. However, in 2011, the *Washington Post* revealed that Rubio's parents had actually obtained permanent U.S. residency more than two years before Castro took power. Rubio quietly amended his Senate biography to reflect the correct timeline.

Still, Rubio's image as a rags-to-political-riches figure resonated across party lines. In 2011, while delivering a speech at the Ronald Reagan Library in California, Rubio helped prevent 90-year-old Nancy Reagan from falling. The act earned him the nickname "knight in shining armour" and reinforced his growing popularity.

In 2013, Rubio's standing with Tea Party conservatives took a hit after he supported a bipartisan immigration reform bill. Though the bill passed the Senate, it failed in the House and Rubio, facing backlash from the right, abandoned the issue.

Rubio launched his presidential campaign in April 2015. His candidacy was heavily funded by Norman Braman, who pledged over $10 million to Rubio's super PAC. Though seen by some Republicans as premature, others viewed him as a promising contender to become America's first Hispanic president.

Ultimately, Donald Trump won the Florida primaries, captured the Republican nomination, and became the 45th President of the United States. Rubio's campaign faltered, but he returned to the Senate with his national profile intact—his future in American politics far from over.

Man of the People or One Man's Fall Guy?

The Secretary of State serves as the President's chief advisor on foreign affairs, tasked with implementing foreign policy through the State Department and U.S. Foreign Service. Key responsibilities include overseeing treaty negotiations, interpreting international agreements, fostering economic relations, and facilitating extradition requests. The Secretary of State is fourth in the presidential line of succession.

Rubio is believed to have vied for the vice presidency, perhaps as part of a longer-term strategy for a second presidential run in 2028. Instead, Trump appointed him to the Cabinet as Secretary of State. On paper, it was a promotion from the Senate, but historically, the role has often been a political cul-de-sac. Cabinet members are rarely credited for successes, such accolades go to the President, yet they remain highly visible targets when policy fails.

With Trump's second presidency plagued by controversy and chaos, Rubio's acceptance of this role could come at significant personal cost. Should Trump attempt to deflect responsibility for foreign policy blunders, Rubio could find himself cast as the scapegoat, a role that could irreparably damage any future political ambitions.

Some have used Cabinet roles as a graceful exit from frontline politics. But Rubio was only 53 when he accepted the appointment, young by American political standards. In the face of Trump's declining popularity and erratic decision-making, Rubio may already be regretting a move that now threatens to end his career rather than elevate it.

Controversy surfaced early in Rubio's tenure. One major flashpoint came when South Africa's Ambassador to Washington, Ebrahim Rasool, a respected anti-apartheid activist and member of Nelson Mandela's African National Congress was declared persona non grata. Expelling an ambassador is an extraordinary act in diplomatic circles. Rubio shared a social media post implying the decision was linked to an academic talk Rasool had given, which discussed Trump's rollbacks on diversity, immigration, and the shifting racial makeup of the U.S.

Yet, diplomatic tensions with South Africa had been rising well before this event. Trump had already frozen aid to Africa, citing laws he claimed allowed land to be seized from white farmers.

In another controversial move, Rubio welcomed Darren Beattie as Acting Under Secretary of State for Public Diplomacy. Beattie had previously been fired from Trump's White House in 2018 after it was revealed he had spoken at a white nationalist conference. Rubio also supported the appointment of Pete Marocco as director of foreign assistance to USAID. Marocco had secretly met with Balkan officials in 2018 some of whom were under U.S. sanctions, including pro-Russian leader Milorad

Dodik. Dodik had praised Vladimir Putin in 2024 as a friend of "anti-American" values. Marocco was later recorded participating in the January 6 Capitol insurrection, although he was never charged.

Rubio had once been a fierce defender of the U.S. Agency for International Development (USAID). But under Trump, USAID was gutted, an assault carried out in part by Elon Musk, dubbed Trump's "special employee." Rubio remained silent. He also failed to protest when Trump revoked deportation protections for Venezuelans, an act Rubio had previously insisted would amount to a death sentence for those affected.

These silences reflect a dramatic shift. Rubio now endorses, or at the very least tolerates, policies he once vehemently opposed. It remains to be seen how he will respond when he fully realises foreign policy is being dictated entirely from the White House. Will he ever reclaim his former stance on human rights, immigration, or international aid?

After losing the 2016 presidential primaries, Rubio was openly humiliated by Trump. Yet, he survived both politically and personally and has since ingratiated himself with Trump's inner circle. But this proximity has come at a steep cost. Rubio has altered his ideological compass, seemingly in exchange for power and proximity.

Trump's appointment of Rubio was not born of personal affection or shared religious conviction. Rather, it was a calculated move to curry favour with Cuban Americans, Hispanic voters, and younger conservatives; demographics Trump desperately needed. Scratch beneath the surface, however, and a darker motive emerges, revenge. By placing Rubio in a high-risk Cabinet role, Trump may be indulging in a vindictive power play, reminding the world who's really in charge.

Rubio's greatest liability may not be his diminished influence but the threat of Trump's wrath. One tweet or offhand comment could dismantle Rubio's credibility or end his political career. Trump possibly not only saw him as expendable, but also replaceable.

And yet, 2025 has proved even more unpredictable. Rubio was appointed to oversee the now-defunct USAID, placed in charge of the National Archives, and, as of May 1, named Acting National Security Adviser. This came about after former adviser Mike Waltz was ousted amid the now-infamous "Signal group chat" scandal.
(See: Misc. Non-Cabinet Roles – National Security Adviser)

A Family Secret

In 1987, Rubio's brother-in-law, Orlando Cicilia, was arrested for his involvement in a multimillion-dollar drug smuggling operation. Authorities claimed Cicilia helped traffic drugs across the U.S. including to Hawaii and pocketed an estimated $15 million. Despite this, Cicilia appeared on stage with Rubio in 2006 when he was named Speaker of the Florida House, and again in 2010 during his Senate victory speech.

The public remained unaware of Cicilia's past until 2011, when *Univision* investigative reporter Gerardo Reyes broke the story. Rubio's team responded with a forceful campaign to shut it down. Rubio also pressured GOP candidates to boycott *Univision's* 2012 Republican debate. As a result, the debate was handed to rival network *Telemundo*, where it was moderated by José Díaz-Balart, the brother of Rubio's political allies, Lincoln and Mario Díaz-Balart.

Rubio took this media exposé personally. Some have called it a "Cuban thing," a reference to the cultural trait of holding deep, long-term grudges. Rubio's retaliation may have backfired as by 2015, *Univision* had become the most-watched network among Hispanic viewers, a key demographic the GOP was eager to reach. *Univision* anchor Jorge Ramos gained national attention when he was ejected from a Trump press conference after questioning Trump's stance on immigration and defending the *DREAM Act*. Ramos prophetically later warned in *The New Yorker* that *"Marco Rubio... won't defend the undocumented."*

That warning now seems chillingly predictive as now in 2025, the U.S. is not just deporting undocumented immigrants but also citizens, with many sent to harsh work camps in El Salvador. The country that once inspired Rubio's family to seek refuge is now sending others to a very different fate.

Secretary of the Treasury

Scott Kenneth Homer Bessent – August 21, 1962

Estimated net worth, January 2025 - $700 Million

Scott Bessent, his husband, former New York City prosecutor John Freeman, and their two children primarily reside in Charleston, South Carolina. In 2025, Bessent became the first Senate-approved LGBTQ+ member in a Republican Cabinet, making him the highest-ranking openly LGBTQ+ person in U.S. history.

In a 2015 interview with *Yale Alumni Magazine*, Bessent reflected on the legalisation of gay marriage: *"In a certain geographic region at a certain economic level, being gay is not an issue... If you had told me in 1984, when we graduated, and people were dying of AIDS, that 30 years later I'd be legally married and we would have two children via surrogacy, I wouldn't have believed you."*

The Early Years

Bessent, the eldest of three children, was raised in Conway, South Carolina. His family, of prominent standing, traces its lineage to the 17th-century French Huguenots*, Protestant refugees who migrated to the Carolinas seeking religious freedom. His father, Homer Gaston Bessent Jr., was a real estate developer; his mother, Barbara McLeod Bessent, played a central role in raising the family.

(*Huguenots were French Protestants who faced religious persecution in France and sought refuge in the Americas.)

After graduating from Yale University in 1984 with a Bachelor of Arts in political science, Bessent began his financial career at Brown Brothers Harriman and later joined Kynikos Associates.

By 1991, Bessent had risen to the position of managing partner at the London-based Soros Fund Management, led by billionaire George Soros. Soros made his name during the 1992 "Black Wednesday" crisis when he helped engineer a $1 billion profit by short-selling the British pound, forcing it out of the European Exchange Rate Mechanism. Soros would become known as "the man who broke the Bank of England."

While based in London, Bessent became an early benefactor of the Prince of Wales Foundation and formed connections with Prince (now King) Charles and Camilla Parker Bowles (now Queen Camilla). He played a principal role in organising Camilla's groundbreaking 1999 U.S. visit, a key moment in reintroducing her to the international stage.

After leaving Soros Fund Management in 2000, Bessent launched his own hedge fund, Bessent Capital, which closed in 2005. Between 2006 and 2010, he served as an adjunct professor at Yale University, teaching economic history, and worked as a senior investment adviser for Protégé Partners.

In 2011, Bessent married John Freeman. Their children, Cole and Caroline, were born via surrogacy. That same year, George Soros brought Bessent back to manage his

$30 billion family office* as Chief Investment Officer. In 2015, Soros provided $2 billion to help Bessent establish a new fund, Key Square Management Group, which was managing approximately $600 million by the end of 2023. The $2 billion loan from Soros was eventually returned as outside investors joined the fund.

*(*A family office is a private firm managing the wealth and affairs of a high-net-worth individual or family.)*

Today, Bessent is believed to be one of the largest private agricultural landowners in North Dakota. He serves as a trustee of Rockefeller University and the Classical American Homes Preservation Trust. His appointment to the Treasury placed him at the epicentre of American economic policymaking.

Political Ascension

Bessent was once a staunch Democrat. In 2000, he hosted a fundraiser for Al Gore and donated to both Hillary Clinton and Barack Obama. However, by 2016, he had realigned his loyalties, donating $1 million to Donald Trump's presidential inauguration committee. His transition toward Republican politics is thought to have been prompted by dissatisfaction with the Biden administration's economic policies.

While attending a financial conference in Hong Kong shortly after Steve Bannon left the Trump White House in 2017, Bessent initiated a conversation that would shape his political future. He later contacted Trump's former chief strategist Bannon, for guidance on how to position himself as a future Treasury Secretary. Bannon's advice: immerse yourself in Trump's economic worldview and learn how to appeal to the MAGA base.

Bessent did just that. He cultivated relationships with Trump's economic inner circle, including Peter Navarro, Larry Kudlow, and Kevin Hassett. He became a frequent guest on right-wing media platforms such as Bannon's *War Room* podcast and *Breitbart News Saturday*, aligning himself with nationalist economic rhetoric.

By 2021, Bessent was publicly defending Trump's controversial use of tariffs, stating on *Fox News* that they were not inflationary but rather a *"useful negotiation tool"* that could bolster Treasury revenues. He contended that the U.S., as the world's largest importer, held the upper hand in trade negotiations and needed only to assert its power.

As Trump's 2024 campaign gained momentum, Bessent emerged as a top donor, fundraiser, and economic adviser. He introduced Trump to Japan's "Three Arrows" economic model, an approach championed by former Japanese Prime Minister Shinzo Abe that prioritised aggressive monetary policy, flexible fiscal spending, and structural reform.

In early 2024, Bessent's hedge fund, Key Square Management, issued a client note suggesting that a surge in U.S. equities reflected the market's anticipation of Trump's return, and not confidence in Biden's economic policies. The memo caught Trump's attention. Soon after,

Bessent was flying aboard Trump's private jet, attending campaign rallies, and rubbing shoulders with Trump insiders like Donald Trump Jr. and Senator J.D. Vance.

Bessent outmanoeuvred prominent contenders for the Treasury role, including asset management firm Apollo Global's Marc Rowan, former Federal Governor Kevin Warsh, and Tennessee Senator Bill Hagerty. Trump's transition co-chair, Howard Lutnick, long seen as the frontrunner, was instead nominated to lead the Commerce Department.

Trump formally announced Bessent's nomination for Treasury Secretary in a November 2024 statement: *"Scott will support my policies that will drive U.S. competitiveness and stop unfair trade imbalances."*

Bessent had managed a rare political balancing act, earning the confidence of Wall Street, gaining traction with MAGA loyalists, and, most critically, convincing Trump of his loyalty.

Bessent has publicly vowed that the Trump administration would not cut Social Security or Medicare, nor would it introduce a central bank digital currency. He also insisted Trump's economic policies would not be inflationary. With economic indicators trending in the opposite direction, Bessent may soon need to re-evaluate these claims.

Time will reveal whether Bessent is a visionary guiding the nation through economic turbulence or a hedge fund opportunist whose greatest investment was in Donald Trump.

One of the Boys: Money Talks

As Secretary of the Treasury, Scott Bessent is fifth in line to the presidency and serves as the highest-ranking economic official in the United States. His department holds the enormous responsibility of managing the world's largest economy, overseeing the collection of taxes, paying the government's bills, and balancing the $36 trillion Treasury debt market.

The Treasury also regulates financial markets, administers U.S. sanctions policy, and conducts national security screenings of foreign investments. It influences global institutions such as the International Monetary Fund and the World Bank. The role, especially under current conditions, is not just influential it is ominously powerful.

Bessent brings to the post over four decades of global financial expertise, particularly in currency markets. Throughout his career, he has built lasting relationships with economic leaders and central bankers, sharpening the diplomatic and negotiation skills vital to managing sensitive topics like sanctions on Russia or navigating complex trade relationships with China, Canada, and Mexico.

His appointment was no accident. Bessent's longstanding association with Trump, combined with deep ties to major Wall Street players, paved a political pathway that few could have predicted a decade earlier. He has been an outspoken supporter of Trump's economic agenda: from the extension of the 2017 tax cuts to controversial tariffs and a shift toward private-sector-led economic expansion.

According to sources close to the administration, Trump was seeking a Treasury Secretary who could bridge two divergent worlds, Wall Street's elite and the populist, MAGA-driven electoral base. The ideal candidate would embrace cryptocurrency, aggressively pursue tariffs, and support immigration crackdowns. In Bessent, he found all of this. A man who not only adapted to the shifting political winds but anticipated them.

Bessent transitioned from Democrat fundraiser to trusted Republican donor. He aligned himself with Trump's closest economic advisers, made himself visible in conservative media, and won the confidence of Trump's inner circle. In short, Bessent didn't just play the game, he mastered it.

As the administration barrels forward with ambitious economic policies, Bessent lends crucial credibility. Wall Street trusts him. Congress respects his competence. Trump believes in his loyalty. Yet the road ahead is treacherous: a rapidly weakening U.S. economy, a ballooning debt, and a volatile international climate threaten to derail even the most seasoned official. With Treasury debt reaching $36 trillion in March 2025, the question is no longer whether Bessent can deliver, but whether anyone can.

From a young age, Bessent had a clear vision of public service. At just 17, when his family was facing serious financial difficulties, he applied for a position at the U.S. Naval Academy. Despite a recommendation from a Carolina Congressman, he was denied entry, because he was gay.

Later, while attending Yale, he encountered more barriers. After graduation, he explored a future in the U.S. State Department, only to discover again that his sexual orientation rendered him unwelcome.

His rise is all the more remarkable in light of these early exclusions. But now, as the first openly gay Cabinet member in a Republican administration, Bessent is in uncharted and potentially precarious territory.

This is the same administration where Speaker of the House Mike Johnson's zealous religious views dominate conservative discourse, and where Defence Secretary Pete Hegseth has pledged to purge all LGBTQ+ and transgender military personnel in a sweeping dismantling of Diversity, Equity, and Inclusion (DEI) programs. Trump's team has backed policies restricting the rights of transgender athletes and banning transgender individuals from using public facilities that match their gender identity.

Given these ideological headwinds, one must ask: is Bessent's presence in the Cabinet a bridge too far for the religious right? Or will his lineage, wealth, and deeply embedded connections allow him to sidestep the prejudices that continue to shape U.S. politics?

Bessent has previously remarked that at a certain level of economic status, being gay "is not an issue." That may be true in elite financial circles but Washington, under Trump in 2025, is a different arena entirely.

Time will tell whether Bessent is merely tolerated for his usefulness or whether his appointment signals a deeper, if uneasy, shift in conservative politics. For now, he remains a critical player in Trump's government, one who has defied expectations and defied the odds. But in a Cabinet where loyalty is paramount and ideology volatile, even his status may not guarantee long-term survival.

Secretary of Defense

Peter Brian Hegseth – June 6, 1980

Estimated net worth, March 2025 - $2 to 6 Million

On March 15, 2025, Secretary of Defense Pete Hegseth confirmed the security status of a 'Signal' group chat discussing "attack plans" to strike Houthi targets in Yemen. In a text message, he stated: *"We are currently clean on OPSEC*"*
However, respected editor-in-chief for *The Atlantic magazine*, Jeffrey Goldberg, had been mistakenly included in the chat.

After the incidence became public knowledge Hegseth's emotionally charged response to questioning by *Fox News* about the Signal chat was: *"... You're talking about a deceitful and highly discredited so-called journalist who's made a profession of peddling hoaxes time and time again."* He continued, *"To include the, I don't know, the hopes of Russia, Russia, Russia, or the fine people on both sides hoaxes or suckers and losers' hoaxes."* Intensifying his attack on Goldberg: *"This is the guy that peddles in garbage. This is what he does,"* Hegseth retorted.

(*OPSEC: Operational Security)

The Early Years

Hegseth was the first of three boys born to Brian and Penelope Hegseth. His father, Brian, was a basketball coach for high schools across Minnesota before retiring in

2019, while his mother, Penny, was an executive business coach. Raised in Forest Lake, Minnesota, Hegseth attended Forest Lake Area High School, where he graduated as valedictorian in 1999 and was later inducted into the school's hall of fame.

Hegseth went on to study at Princeton University, where he earned a Bachelor of Arts degree in Politics. He also gained certificates from the School for Public and International Affairs and American Studies. During his time at Princeton, Hegseth was the publisher and writer for *The Princeton Tory*, the university's main conservative publication. There, he developed an enthusiasm for studying the Western Canon*, though his controversial comments on diversity, feminism, and LGBTQ+ issues often sparked outrage.

(*Western Canon: A collection of literary, artistic, and musical works regarded as the most important and influential in shaping Western culture.)

In 2002, under Hegseth's leadership, *The Princeton Tory* published a mocking article aimed at pride events on campus: *"Hey, boys can wear bras and girls can wear ties until we're blue in the face, but it won't change the reality that the homosexual lifestyle is abnormal and immoral."* Hegseth himself dismissed critics of conservatives as intolerant, advocating for government support for the traditional family unit, freedom from government oversight, and asserted that the revival of religious faith provided a blueprint for a free and prosperous future.

Hegseth was also a varsity basketball player, the recipient of a Witherspoon Fellowship from the Family Research Council and served as a company commander in the Reserve Officer's Training Corps (ROTC): a university-based officer training program that helps pay for college tuition in exchange for a commitment to four years of active-duty service after graduation.

After graduating from 'Princeton' in 2003, Hegseth joined Bear Stearns, an investment bank on Wall Street. But soon after, his Army National Guard unit was activated, and within a week, he was deploying to Guantanamo Bay, Cuba. From 2005 to 2006, Hegseth served in Iraq as an infantry platoon leader, later becoming a civil-military operations officer. He earned a Bronze Star and a Combat Infantryman Badge for his service.

In 2012, Hegseth volunteered to deploy to Afghanistan as a captain in the Minnesota Army National Guard. His role was to train Afghan security forces and prepare them to take over regional security responsibilities. After leaving active duty in 2014, he was promoted to the rank of major and assigned to the Army Individual Ready Reserve.

In 2014, Hegseth transitioned to a career in political commentary with *Fox News*, eventually becoming a weekend co-host for *Fox & Friends Weekend* from 2017 to 2024. Alongside this, he completed a postgraduate Master of Arts in Public Policy from Harvard University in 2013. Despite this prestigious degree, he often criticised Harvard and its curriculum. In one notable incident on *Fox & Friends*, he described his time at the university as filled with "pointless" studies such as government and climate change. Hegseth mocked Ivy League diversity initiatives and, in an on-air stunt, wrote "return to sender" on his Harvard degree.

Throughout his career, Hegseth has been outspoken on issues related to transgender rights, women's rights, and LGBTQ+ military service members. He has insinuated that the inclusion of these individuals in the military deters potential recruits. In his 2024 book, *The War on Warriors: Behind the Betrayal of the Men Who Keep Us Free*, he wrote, *"The shoehorning of... DEI, Critical Race Theory, feminism, genderism, "safetyism", climate worship, manufactured violent extremism, straight-up weirdo shit, and a grab bag of social justice causes that infect today's fighting force have nothing to do with making our military capable."* His exclusionary stance, focusing narrowly on a particular "warrior" ideal, paints a picture of a man who is uncompromising and intolerant.

Political Ascension

Hegseth's rise in the political world began in 2007 when he became the executive director of American political advocacy group Vets for Freedom. However, by 2012, financial mismanagement led to his departure. During this time, he also gained visibility through frequent media appearances, newspaper editorials, and public speaking engagements, positioning himself as a prominent political figure. After his final overseas deployment to Afghanistan in 2012, Hegseth filed paperwork to run for Minnesota's U.S. Senate seat.

His Senate campaign focused on his strong family values, with his parents appearing in promotional materials praising his loyalty and devotion to his wife and son. However, after failing to gain his party's endorsement, he dropped out after just three months. Throughout his Senate bid, Hegseth continued to gain recognition within conservative circles, including through leadership roles in nonprofit veteran's groups aligned with the Republican Party.

Hegseth's talent for finding the spotlight made him a recognised figure in media and political circles, eventually leading him to a role as a *Fox News* contributor in 2014. His prominence continued to grow in 2015, when he hosted multiple town hall forums with presidential candidates. However, his tenure with a second American political advocacy group, Concerned Veterans for America, (2013–2016) ended amidst accusations of financial mismanagement, sexual impropriety, and alcohol-related incidents.

After President Donald Trump's 2016 election, Hegseth sought a position in Trump's administration, interviewing three times for the role of Secretary of Veterans Affairs. Although unsuccessful, Hegseth's efforts did not go unnoticed, and he remained a trusted figure within conservative circles.

Although Hegseth was not an immediate Trump supporter, criticising Trump's veteran policy in 2015 in favour of other Republican candidates like Marco Rubio and Ted Cruz, he underwent a conversion moment, aligning himself firmly with Trump after the 2016 election. His role at *Fox News* gave him a platform to defend Trump and attack the media, Democrats, and the special counsel investigating Russian interference in the 2016 election.

For the next eight years, Hegseth worked diligently to cultivate relationships within the Republican Party and promote his chosen narrative. He published two controversial books, *American Crusade* (2020) and *The War on Warriors* (2024), made frequent public speaking appearances and solidified his place as a key *Fox News* host. By 2022, Hegseth became involved with the Communion of Reformed Evangelical Churches, a group that espouses extreme Christian theology and supports MAGA Christianity. The church promotes patriarchal traditions and a belief in re-establishing biblical law, viewing women's roles as limited to homemaking and family.

After years of aligning with conservative ideologies, Hegseth meticulously crafted a resume that he hoped would position him for a chance to be nominated for Secretary of Defense. While President Trump touted

Hegseth's Harvard education as an elite qualification for the role, the irony of Hegseth's earlier rejection of the institution's teachings raises questions about his qualifications for such a complex and critical position. The expertise, diplomacy, and nuanced understanding required to lead the U.S. Department of Defense seem glaringly absent from Hegseth's background. His rise from *Fox TV* host to Secretary of Defense highlights the influence of connections, wealth, and political compliance in the American political system.

Traditional Family Values

Hegseth married his Minnesota high school sweetheart, Meredith Schwarz, in 2004 at the Cathedral of Saint Paul in Minnesota. The marriage lasted only five years. It ended after Hegseth admitted to engaging in multiple (five) affairs during their relationship. Perplexingly, Hegseth's extramarital affairs and subsequent divorce occurred at the same time he was constructing his conservative credentials, highlighting "traditional family values" as a core belief.

Hegseth was a guest speaker at a 2006 event organised by the Family Research Council (FRC), an evangelical non-profit activist group and think tank that provided him with his 'Witherspoon Fellowship' at Princeton. The FRC's philosophy on marriage, family, and sexuality, outlined on their website, states they *"champion marriage and family as the foundational cornerstone of civilization, the seedbed of virtue, and the wellspring of society. Properly understood, 'families' are formed only by ties of blood, marriage, or adoption, and 'marriage' is a union of one man and one woman. The only appropriate context for sexual relations is within the marriage of a man and a woman. Moreover, we believe that because God created us 'male and female' (Gen. 5:2), we have no right to re-create ourselves otherwise."* The FRC is an outspoken advocate for bans on abortion and same-sex marriage and regularly engages in policy discussions about the harms of divorce.

Hegseth's first wife, Meredith, filed for divorce in December 2008. By that time, he was already dating Samantha Deering, whom he had met while working in Washington, D.C. at Vets for Freedom (2007–2012). In 2010, Hegseth married Samantha, and together they had three children: Gunner, Boone, and Rex, building what appeared to be a stable family life. However, cracks began to show as Hegseth once again tested the limits of the very values he espoused. He began a relationship with Jennifer Rauchet, then a married senior producer at *Fox News*, who became pregnant with his child. The affair became public in 2017, effectively ending his second marriage. His divorce from Samantha, the mother of his three sons, was finalised later that year.

Nevertheless, Hegseth's fourth child, Gwen, was born in 2017, prior to his marriage to Jennifer Rauchet in 2019. The ceremony was held at Trump National Golf Club in Colts Neck, New Jersey. Rauchet, a television producer known for her work at *Fox News*, is also a mother of three from two previous marriages.

In a December 2024 interview on *The Megyn Kelly Show*, Hegseth confirmed he had sexual relations with another woman in 2017 while in a relationship with Rauchet, just two months after their child was born. This encounter resulted in a sexual assault accusation. While no formal charges were filed, Hegseth did reach a monetary settlement with his accuser. He stated, *"Being in a hotel room with someone that's not the person you're with is not okay. I own up to that, and I've had to own up to that, and that's been difficult, and my wife's amazing, and you know she knew about it, but going through it again is not easy."*

Despite this, Hegseth has continually marketed himself as a defender of traditional family values, declaring that conservatives should focus on reducing divorce. *"The focus on family policy should... be on strengthening families and creating good citizens by preventing divorce of parents with kids, encouraging large productive families...,"* he wrote in his 2016 book *In the Arena*. By 2017, a revised edition of the book had softened this message, narrowing the focus to preventing only "wanton divorce."

(Hypocrite: someone who puts on a false appearance of virtue or religion; one who acts in contradiction to their stated beliefs.)

The Frontline Face of U.S. Defence

The Office of the Secretary of Defense (OSD) is responsible for the development of policy, planning, resource management, and evaluation of defense programs. As Secretary of Defense, Hegseth oversees the Department of Defense (DoD) and serves as its chief policy advisor and strategist. The OSD also functions as the civilian leadership hub within the DoD, encompassing key figures responsible for strategic decisions in defense policy and operations.

Hegseth has expressed disdain for the Geneva Conventions*, rules of engagement, and treaties designed to constrain military actions and uphold the laws of war.

(*Geneva Conventions: A universally ratified set of international treaties that establish a minimum standard for the humane treatment of individuals during war.)

He appears incapable of grasping the moral implications of warfare and shows little to no empathy for its victims. In his 2024 book *War on Warriors...*, Hegseth reflected on the U.S. atomic bombings of Japan during World War II, writing, *"They won. Who cares."* I care, Pete. I care.

(*On August 6, 1945, the U.S. dropped the first atomic bomb on Hiroshima. Three days later, a second bomb was dropped on Nagasaki. By the end of 1945, an estimated 210,000 people had died from the blasts, burns, and radiation.*)

Hegseth frequently shares his opinion that women in combat make units less capable. Despite combat roles opening to women in 2016 under Defense Secretary Ash Carter, and numerous women successfully passing the military's gruelling tests to become Green Berets, Army Rangers, and Naval Special Warfare crew members, Hegseth argues that diversity only strengthens the military when it includes minorities and white men, excluding combat-trained military women from this category.

The role of Secretary of Defense has, under this administration, been reduced to what many see as an entry-level position. But with Trump's preference for spectacle, it's no surprise he was drawn to Hegseth's image: a telegenic military veteran with a reputation for disruption. Hegseth represents the ideal MAGA warrior, aggressive, influential, and eager to fight. He is another loyalist Trump believes will follow orders without question.

Hegseth has no political experience beyond a failed 2012 campaign for a U.S. Senate seat. But Trump values performative loyalty over policy expertise. In many ways, Hegseth is Trump's "Mini-me." * He echoes Trump's most extreme views, lashes out at media scrutiny, and refuses to apologise for offensive or controversial behaviour. And like 'Mini-me,' he appears a little unhinged.

(*Mini-me is a fictional character from the second and third Austin Powers films. He is a clone of the villain Dr. Evil.)

With his appetite for conflict and disdain for Washington's power structures, Hegseth embodies the Trump administration's chaotic ethos. He markets himself as a Pentagon outsider who will challenge the status quo. To MAGA populists, he is a relatable figure, someone who shares their rage and desire to tear down institutions they believe have failed them.

Yet the position of Secretary of Defense is far from symbolic. It requires managing a $900 billion budget, providing oversight for millions of military personnel and their families, and advising the president on the use of military force.

Pete Hegseth, now Secretary of Defense, is a Trumpian loyalist at best and a global disaster waiting to happen at worst.

Hegseth has a documented history of sexual misconduct and inappropriate professional behaviour. His views on women's roles in the military, and their impact on the over 200,000 women in active service who put their lives on the line, are abhorrent.

In his 2020 book *American Crusade,'* Hegseth wrote: *"The defense of Europe is not our problem; been there, done that, twice,"* adding, *"NATO is a relic and should be scrapped and remade in order for freedom to be truly defended."* He also described the United Nations as *"a fully globalist organisation that aggressively advances an anti-American, anti-Israel, and anti-freedom agenda."*

This is not the ideal mindset of a man who heads the world's most powerful military—and who advises the president in control of a vast nuclear arsenal.

Attorney General

Pamela Jo Bondi – November 17, 1965

Estimated net worth, March 2025 - $10 Million

In her first month in office, Bondi, set about clearing the Department of Justice (DOJ) of employees she saw as unsupportive of Trump, announced that the DOJ would stop DEI Programs it considered illegal, and cease federal funding to sanctuary cities*. She supported the dismissal of corruption charges against New York City (sanctuary city) Mayor Eric Adams, arguing the case was limiting Adams's ability to enforce Trump's crackdown on illegal immigration. This support started the most significant groundswell of resignations by career prosecutors since the Nixon era Watergate scandal.

(*Sanctuary city; places that limit enforcement of federal immigration laws in order to protect undocumented immigrants).

The Early Years

Bondi and her two siblings were born in Temple Terrace, Florida to her mother Patsy Loretta (née Hammer) and her father Joseph Bondi. Her mother was an elementary school teacher, and her father was a professor and also served as mayor of their hometown between 1974 to 1978. In 1983 Bondi graduated from C. Leon King High School in Tampa. She then completed a Bachelor of Arts degree in criminal justice at the University of Florida in 1987, before completing a Juris

Doctor degree at Stetson University's College of Law in 1990. After gaining her Juris Doctor degree Bondi married Garret Barnes however the marriage ended in divorce just under 2 years later.

She was admitted to the Florida Bar in 1991 and began her career as a prosecutor in Hillsborough County, managing high-profile cases, including those involving public figures and controversial legal matters. Bondi married Scott Fitzgerald in 1996, they later divorced in 2002. Bondi was a prosecutor in the state attorney's office in Hillsborough County, Florida for 18 years. She was well regarded for her friendly style in the courtroom and was proficient at connecting with jurors. Branching out as a legal analyst, Bondi also undertook court commentary positions for *Fox News* and *CNN*.

In 2010, she ran for the position of Florida Attorney General. Former Alaskan governor and vice-presidential candidate Sarah Palin endorsed Bondi for this role. Palin's endorsement elevated Bondi's standing in the primary elections leading to her becoming the 37th and first female Attorney General in Florida's history. She went on to serve for two consecutive terms from 2011 to 2019, prioritising issues such as reducing drug abuse, putting an end to human trafficking, and advocating against the Obama administration's signature health care plan, the Affordable Care Act (ACA).

Bondi received nationwide attention for her opposition to the ACA and her stance against same-sex marriage laws. Conversely, she also established a reputation for championing animal welfare issues and was instrumental in fighting for a ballot measure banning greyhound racing in the state and shutting down puppy mills.

In 2012, she became engaged to ophthalmologist Dr. Greg Henderson. However, the relationship did not eventuate in marriage and since 2017, she has been in a relationship with John Wakefield, a founding principal of VW Multifamily, a real estate private equity company centered on investments in Florida and the Carolinas.

Political Ascension

Bondi has been a longtime and early ally of Trump. While serving as attorney general for Florida she utilised her appearances on *Fox News* to defend Trump and his policies gaining national attention for her stance. In March 2016, she endorsed Trump at a rally, choosing him over her home state candidate, Florida Senator Marco Rubio. This notoriety led to a prestigious speaking appearance at the 2016 Republican National Convention where Trump was officially named the party's presidential nominee.

Even after she left the attorney general's office, she stayed in Trump's sphere of influence serving as a chairwoman of the America First Policy Institute, think tank. This connection continued after Trump's first term ended with her continuing to help Trump's former staff members to organise in readiness for a possible second term in office for Trump.

After her second term as attorney general ended in 2019, and Bondi could not legally seek a third term in office, she took a position as a corporate lobbyist with Ballard Partners, a powerful lobby firm. Trump's former campaign chief and current Whitehouse chief of staff, Susie Wiles, was at that time a managing partner at Ballard Partners Jacksonville office and its founder, Brain Ballard is a notable fundraiser for Trump.

Bondi lobbied for an impressive list of clients in her time at Ballard Partners including General Motors, the government of Qatar in relation to anti-human-trafficking efforts leading up to the 2022 World Cup, and a Kuwaiti firm lobbying the White House, National Security Council, State Department and Congress on immigration policy, human rights and economic sanctions issues.

Bondi served as one of Trump's defense lawyers during his first impeachment trial in 2020 and by 2024 was running the legal branch of the Trump affiliated America First Policy Institute. A long-time vocal critic of the many criminal cases against Trump, Bondi targeted Special Counsel Jack Smith who pressed charges against Trump in two of his cases, labelling him and other prosecutors as horrible people who were just trying to make a name for themselves.

Bondi's ties to Trump were raised during her Senate confirmation hearing for the position of attorney general. Concerns about the potential for political interference in the DOJ were raised. She gave the Senate her assurances that she would maintain the departments independence, affirming, *"I will not inject politics into criminal or civil investigations."* However, critics still held valid concerns about punitive actions aimed at Trump's political antagonists.

Nonpartisan Law Enforcer or Trump Beholden?

As Attorney General, Bondi holds the position of the top U.S. federal law enforcement officer in charge of the U.S. DOJ. Her main duties are legal advisor to the President and heads of executive departments, ensuring compliance with federal laws, supervision of federal prosecutors, managing legal issues related to public safety, national security, and civil rights.

The position encompasses the Supervision and administration of the Federal Bureau of Investigation, Drug Enforcement Administration, Bureau of Alcohol, Tobacco, Firearms and Explosives, Bureau of Prisons, Office of Justice Programs and the U.S. Attorneys and U.S. Marshals Service, as these all come under the umbrella of the Department of Justice.

During the Senate confirmation process Bondi was praised for her accomplishments in her career and her level of competency for the role of Attorney General. There appears to be very little doubt that Bondi was a capable and experienced nominee for the attorney general position. Nevertheless, Senators who opposed her nomination voiced concerns about the influence

Trump could have on Bondi's vision and choice of direction for the DOJ. The concerns centred around her resolute loyalty to Trump, and other party allies, and whether this loyalty could blur Bondi's objectivity if she were ever forced to have to choose between loyalty and the letter of the law.

It would appear Bondi's loyalty to her sponsors may have been tested on an earlier occasion as in 2011 two attorneys in the Florida attorney general's office, June Clarkson and Theresa Edwards, were fired. As part of their work for Florida's Economic Crime Division, Clarkson and Edwards had been investigating a housing foreclosure scandal involving financial services company, Lender Processing Services (LPS). The attorneys had uncovered many law firms across Florida that were using phony documents to speed up foreclosures on homeowners during the Global Financial Crisis housing bubble. During the GFC banks and lenders were securitising loans without keeping the chain of title, effectively trashing the real ownership records, and then on-selling the mortgages to investors. Instead of fixing the situation the banks had the law firms prepare false evidence that was presented to the courts to dispossess people. Documents were found that were signed "Bogus Assignee," dated 9/9/9999 and notarised on dates prior to their date of creation. Clarkson and Edwards obtained evidence from a former paralegal with one of the suspect law firms, who testified that foreclosure document outlets in Guam and the Philippines were used to produce fake documents that were then signed and falsely notarised by the paralegals. Due to this investigation all of the leading banks, by October 2010, ceased pursuing foreclosures both in Florida and across the U.S. because it had been found to be illegal.

In 2010 Bondi won the election as Florida attorney general, thanks in no small part to contributions from LPS and its associates, starting her tenure in early 2011. Attorneys Clarkson and Edwards were later stopped from taking part in the ongoing attorney general investigation of foreclosure fraud, even though they were the most knowledgeable of any prosecutors in the country. By May 2011, Clarkson and Edwards were fired, without explanation. After they left, no other subpoenas were issued by the attorney general's department to any foreclosure firms or their associates with several ongoing investigations closed without any charges being laid. Several top deputies from the attorney general's office went on to assume senior executive positions at LPS and other foreclosure mills.

Further in 2013, her Florida office was reviewing complaints and considering joining the New York attorney general's office in a case that involved at least 22 fraud allegations against the, now failed, Trump University. This was also the time Bondi was preparing to run for her second term as attorney general. Trump donated $25 thousand to her campaign. Bondi's office decided to drop the case against Trump citing lack of evidence and some months later Trump kindly held a fundraiser for Bondi's re-election campaign at Mar-a-Lago. Trump and Bondi denied any wrongdoing.

Three separate lawsuits were filed against Trump University alleging Trump University had defrauded its students and only days before being sworn in as president in 2017, Trump was ordered by the courts to pay a $25 million settlement.

Additionally, the role of the attorney general includes being available on the date of executions in case any last-minute legal issues arise. Bondi, in 2013, exhibited a blatant disregard for the judicial process when she sought to delay the execution of a convicted killer as the date for the execution conflicted with a fundraiser for her re-election campaign. Requesting a postponement of this kind for personal gain is morally and ethically reprehensible. Bondi later, in a public apology, stated she was sorry for requesting the Governor push back the execution of Marshall Lee Gore by three weeks.

Bondi's first day in office was a whirlwind of orders designed to realign the DOJ's priorities. A task force concentrating on the seizure of money from Russian oligarchs, an FBI effort to counter foreign influence operations on social media were disbanded and enforcement of the *Foreign Agents Registration Act* that governs whether U.S. corporations can pay bribes overseas were curtailed. Many of the programs abolished or relegated were ones that Trump and his allies had previously maintained were improperly used to investigate them. Several prosecutors who had previously worked on the criminal investigations of Trump, were let go and the Public Integrity Section, that for decades, had focused on prosecuting political corruption and had been involved in the cases against Trump was dramatically downsized.

At least a dozen of the most senior career public servants at the department were removed from their national security and criminal divisions jobs and were offered positions in a working group acting against sanctuary cities. Some stayed, some left. Sections of the DOJ and the FBI were reassigned to target illegal immigrants and Mexican drug cartels even though some of these had previously been involved in fighting terrorism and organised crime syndicates.

It would appear Trump's second attempt at controlling the Justice Department may be somewhat more successful than his first.

Trump's first choice for U.S. Attorney General was Matt Gaetz. However, Gaetz withdrew himself from the running after a federal sex trafficking investigation and ethics probe made his ability to be confirmed untenable. Within hours Trump had chosen Bondi.

Bondi boasted on *Fox News* about her enduring and close relationship with Trump and her pride at carrying out his wishes. This included firing prosecutors who worked on Trump's criminal charges case even though many of them had distinguished Justice Department careers. She emphasised Special Counsel Jack Smith who had led the team of prosecutors, saying, *"The Jack Smith team, gone,"* and more blatantly, *"That was low hanging fruit. Get rid of them, get rid of the people that raided Mar-a-Lago."*

The firing of DOJ attorneys Clarkson and Edwards in 2011 could be interpreted as an early sign of Bondi's willingness to do the bidding of her benefactors. No doubt, she has the career qualifications to be Attorney General, but the ultimate qualification required to be chosen by Trump is unwavering loyalty and all the better if they have also "seen the light" and stepped over to the Trump side.

Bondi aced the Donald Trump Attorney loyalty test, by hawking lies about a stolen election, asserting that she will prosecute Trump's alleged enemies, and re-arranging the staff and priorities of the DOJ. These actions should raise significant apprehensions about the ongoing independence of the Justice Department and the separation of powers between levels of government.

With Bondi's deep ties to Trump, her leadership is set to be closely watched. Her ability to balance legal integrity with political pressures, or lack thereof, will define her legacy.

Several Justice Department officials have been reported as saying that there is now a widespread understanding within the agency that people sympathetic to Trump's politics are being elevated to senior jobs.

Over the last five decades, the Justice Department has striven to adopt policies and norms specifically designed to separate the institution from the impact of political pressure from a sitting president. Attorneys general of both political parties have striven to emphasise that they are not the president's lawyer. They are the representative of the people of the United States.

Secretary of the Interior

Douglas James Burgum – August 1st, 1956

Estimated net worth, February 2025 - $100 Million

Doug Burgum, in his time as governor of Dakota, was well respected as being unafraid to ruffle feathers with the right leaning members of his party. An independent thinking businessman not consumed by partisan politics.

The 2025 public image of Burgum as a steadfast defender of Trump is counterintuitive to the Burgum his constituents and fellow business owners once knew.

The Early Years

Born in Arthur, Dakota, a town with a population of just 300, Doug Burgum grew up surrounded by farmland and a powerful sense of belonging. His family connections to the area can be traced back to 1870. He is one of three children of Katherine (née Kilbourne) Burgum and Joseph Boyd Burgum. His grandfather set up the local grain elevator in 1906. The family still runs the elevator business and Burgum spent his high school years working in the family business.

Burgum was well liked and popular at high school and competed in several sports including football, basketball and track and field. He gained a Bachelor of University Studies degree from North Dakota State University in Fargo in 1978 and successfully went on to earn an MBA at Stanford University. After completing his studies at Stanford Burgum took a position as a consultant with the

Chicago office of McKinsey & Company. He returned to North Dakota in 1983, when an opportunity arose to invest in a start-up software company, Great Plains Software. To raise the required $250,000 seed capital required, Burgum mortgaged a previously inherited 160-acre family farm. This potentially risky venture would turn out to be a very wise investment.

Burgum married his first wife, Karen Stoker, in 1991. They had three children, two sons and a daughter, together before divorcing in 2003. He married former CEO of Longhorn Marketing in Fargo, Kathryn (née Helgaas) Burgum in 2016. Kathryn, who is a recovering alcoholic, is a nationally recognised advocate for addiction recovery who works to end the shame and stigma of the chronic disease of addiction in North Dakota's communities.

Great Plains Software grew into a notable player in the business accounting software market and in 1997, with a valuation of over $200 million, went public. And in 2001, Microsoft acquired it for $1.1 billion. The acquisition by Microsoft included Burgum receiving approximately 1.7 million Microsoft shares, worth roughly $100 million in 2001 dollars. He also took on the role of Senior Vice President of Business Solutions staying on with Microsoft for six years.

Following his departure from Microsoft, Burgum set up a real estate and investment firm centered on reviving downtown Fargo, the most populous city in North

Dakota, and in 2008 co-founded Arthur Ventures, a venture capital firm supporting software companies. He has also held many boards of directors' positions and was a member of the advisory council for the Stanford School of Business.

Political Ascension

Burgum ran for Governor of North Dakota in 2016 winning in a landslide victory. He went on to push for tax cuts, energy production, and infrastructure development and, unlike many other Republicans during the COVID-19 pandemic, he urged Dakota residents to wear masks. He was re-elected for a second term in 2020, strengthening his reputation as a respected leader. North Dakota experienced the highest growth in real GDP and the lowest unemployment rate in the U.S. during Burgum's time as governor. Forbes awarded him the honour of being named "America's Best Entrepreneurial Governor."

Burgum's threw his hat into the ring of national politics in 2023 when he announced his candidacy for the Republican presidential nomination. Despite failing to secure a nomination he used his campaign to reveal his vision for America's future. On the campaign trail he offered himself as a traditional, business-minded conservative rather than a Trump copycat.

However, as his campaign failed, he chose to endorse Trump for the Republican nomination. Burgum went on to play the politics game outstandingly, he made a sizable number of fundraising phone calls, took part in finance meetings and brought in new major donors to Trump's campaign. Burgum was a rich guy who was well connected and could bolster Trump's fundraising. He became an outspoken supporter, appearing on TV news shows and at campaign rallies. He was also, for a time, on Trump's short list of potential candidates for the position of Vice-President. In the same month Burgum was nominated for the Secretary of the Interior position he declined to seek a third term as governor for North Dakota.

It's Just a Step to the Right

Burgum, as Secretary of the Interior and chairman of the newly formed National Energy Council, will be looking to make the most of his unique skill set. The Department of the Interior oversees vast public lands and natural resources and includes 11 varying agencies: the National Park Service, U.S. Fish and Wildlife Service, U.S. Geological Survey, Office of Surface Mining Reclamation and Enforcement, and the bureaus of Indian Affairs, Indian Education, Land Management, Ocean Energy Management, Reclamation, Safety and Environmental Enforcement, and Trust Funds Administration. This position also calls for the overseeing of approximately 70,000 staff and the allocation of an operating budget of around $14 billion. A massive undertaking even though the responsibility lines up with Burgum's personal and professional experiences. Progressing the Trump administration's policies on public lands, energy, the environment and the federal government's relationship with Tribes will also require a diplomatic and strategic skill set.

In the past Burgum was thought of as a moderate, reasonable guy. This reasonableness was apparent in Burgum's efforts, while governor, to improve relations with North Dakota's native American tribes and his vetoes in 2021 of Republican-backed legislation that targeted transgender youth in school sports. Some political allies believe Burgum has only shifted alliance to the right to advance favour with Trump.

Burgum's close ties to oil and gas producers are most plain in his close friendship with billionaire Harold Hamm, founder of Continental Resources, a petroleum and natural gas exploration and production company responsible for much of North Dakota's fracking boom. Hamm advises Trump on energy policy and is thought to have played a role in helping Burgum secure the Department of the Interior position.

However, Trump without doubt appreciates Burgum's strong public-speaking ability, his money, his connections and his expertise in energy and fossil fuel issues. Industry groups welcomed Burgum's inclusion in Trump's new administration and cheered Trump's creation of an energy council signalling revived emphasis on stimulating domestic production and easing the "burden" of regulations. Industry lobby groups were also quick to laud Burgum's understanding of U.S.

energy resources and utilising public lands as they push to strengthen the U.S. in the global energy marketplace.

Tim Purdon a former Democratic U.S. attorney in North Dakota eloquently expressed his views on Burgum's shift to the right when he asserted, *"...he has positioned himself... as the Trumpiest Trumper whoever Trumped."* Purdon also questioned Burgum's motives, *"Does Doug Burgum believe that the election was stolen, and that Donald Trump is truly the greatest president in American history?"* and *"Does he believe that or is he just saying that to gain power? I don't know, but I'll tell you this: I don't know which one of those is worse."*

Secretary of Agriculture

Brooke Christine Leslie (née Clifford) Rollins – April 10, 1972

Estimated net worth, February 2025 - $1 Million

Trump's ongoing policy swings and sweeping trade tariffs will affect farmers and will impact the majority of U.S. citizens. Agriculture secretaries are not usually prominent faces of an administration when things are going smoothly. But when the agricultural industry and the nation's food supply is an issue, it could be another story.

The Early Years

Brooke Rollins grew up in the small agricultural community of Glen Rose, Texas with her parents Helen (née Kerwin) and Hugh Clifford, and is the product of several generations of American farmers. Growing up on the family's farm she gained firsthand experience of rural life and an understanding of the workings of the Texas agricultural industry. During her teen years she was an active member of the youth development program, Texas 4-H, and later served as a state officer for Texas for the National Future Farmers of America (FFA) Organisation.

Rollins gained a degree in agricultural development, graduating with honors, from Texas A&M University and was the first woman to be elected student body president. She went on to earn her Juris Doctor, also with honors, at the University of Texas School of Law and completed a federal judicial clerkship with the Honorable Barbara M.G. Lynn, a U.S. Federal District Judge in the Northern District of Texas. She began her legal career as a litigator at Hughes & Luce, in Dallas.

Texas Governor Rick Perry, (Trump's Energy Secretary between 2016 and 2020), offered Rollins a position in his administration as a deputy general counsel. By 2000 she had worked her way up to the role of policy director, managing the Governor's entire policy portfolio, including agriculture and the natural resources policy agenda. In 2003 she left the governor's office to join the Texas Public Policy Foundation (TPPF), a political policy think tank, where she stayed for the next 15 years.

Rollins became known for her commitment to community issues in the areas of education, agriculture, and criminal justice reform. She held an advisory role, through the TPPF, about the passage of the *First Step Act.* * The Act was hailed as a major step in reforming the criminal justice system. However, the TPPF also championed a Texas-led lawsuit aimed at ending the *Affordable Care Act,* an issue the Republican Party have failed to pass on several occasions. During these advisory sessions Trump showed an interest in the TPPF's litigation efforts and also to the group's ideas on rolling back environmental regulations.

(*First Step Act, 2018, aimed to mitigate the harsh sentencing practices that fuelled the mass incarceration crisis

in the U.S., and introduced critical reforms to improve conditions within federal prisons).

Rollins and her husband, Mark, presently live in Fort Worth, Texas, with their four children and are said to spend a large majority of their free time engaged in community sporting and agricultural groups.

Political Ascension

Rollins first joined Trump's Economic Advisory Council in 2016 while still involved with the TPPF but in 2018, she took on the advisory role of Assistant to the President for Strategic Initiatives in the White House. She went on to administer the White House's Office of American Innovation and the director of the Domestic Policy Council. In 2020 Rollins co-founded the America First Policy Institute (AFPI) alongside former Trump adviser Larry Kudlow. She was the President and Chief Executive Officer of the nonprofit research institute that focused on advancing Trump's first-term agenda after he lost his 2020 re-election bid. The institute also developed policy and developed a network of personnel for Trump's second administration.

Rollins is also a member of the board with the advocacy group America First Works (AFW), a right-wing advocacy arm of the AFPI, whose purpose is to build a team of loyal Patriots and champion the Policies of Trump's America First Agenda. In 2021 Rollin's returned to the TPPF as a senior advisor and a member of the board.

There were several names being bandied around for the Secretary of Agriculture position. Many expected Georgia Senator Kelly Loeffler to be nominated. But after weeks of intense internal fighting among Trump's advisers, family members and powerful agriculture groups Trump chose Brooke Rollins. She was sworn in as the Secretary of Agriculture on February 13, 2025.

Feed the Masses and Serve Trump's Agenda?

Rollins will only be the second woman to oversee the United States Department of Agriculture (USDA). The USDA operates a $430 billion-plus yearly budget and employs 100,000 people and steers nearly every part of the U.S.'s $1.5 trillion food and agriculture industry. A monolithic, complex department, the USDA oversees many agencies and programs, including the Food Safety and Inspection Service (FSIS), the Agricultural Research Service (ARS), and the Natural Resources Conservation Service (NRCS).

Rollins department will additionally be charged with overseeing the 'Supplemental Nutrition Assistance Program,' (SNAP) the U.S.'s largest anti-hunger program. Trump's administration, as part of their 2025 policy agenda, is reducing future spending on the SNAP which provides food aid benefits to more than 40 million low-income Americans. Her influence will also extend to forming agriculture policy and farm subsidy decisions, which are at the heart of the U.S. food system. She will be required to work with Health and Human Services

Secretary Robert F. Kennedy Jr., as he has expressed his eagerness to overhaul the U.S. food system.

The U.S. agriculture sector is facing multiple challenges, including labour shortages exacerbated by mass deportations, trade uncertainties including Trump's propensity for tariffs', and the need for robust rural development. It will be interesting to see how Rollins deals with these issues and remains in line with the Trump administration's unpredictable broader agenda.

A trade war triggered crippling retaliatory tariffs against U.S. farmers during Trump's first term and in his second term he appears intent on waging another tariff war. Rollins is a Trump loyalist who has praised his economic plans. Only time will tell whether she will offer any major resistance to the new rounds of tariffs and if she does, will Trump heed her advice?

Not long after becoming the agriculture secretary Rollins declared, by memo, an "emergency situation determination" across more than 112 million acres of national forest system land. Issued on April 4, 2025, following an executive order aimed toward increasing timber production by 25 per cent, said to be designed to give the U.S. forest service the authority to expediate emergency measures to reduce wildfire risks.

The aim of the determination however may be seeking two very different objectives, increasing forest harvesting by 25% and reducing wildfire risks is not always a compatible strategy*.

(*fire density has been found to be most severe in young forests and declines as forests age. Forests between the ages of approximately seven and eighty years are at a significantly greater risk of severe fires).

Rollins was a surprise pick for the agriculture secretary role as some felt she had less experience in agricultural policy than others on Trump's shortlist. However, she has considerable experience in public policy and administration. Rollins, over many years, has forged a strong relationship with Trump, who prizes proven loyalty in his Cabinet. She has deep ties to Trump's political agenda through the America First Policy Institute think tank, playing a pivotal role in shaping policies for Trump's incoming administration. As he campaigned for a second term Trump faced criticism from former staffers. Rollins stood strong and was among the former aides who were publicly outspoken in Trump's defense.

Rollins has an agricultural background, extensive advocacy and policy advisory experience, she is a well-educated savvy lobbyist who has proven her loyalty to Trump over successive years. She ticks all the boxes to be successful in the role of Secretary of Agriculture, that is, assuming her loyalty to Trump does not override her ability to make principled decisions.

Powerful, conservative-leaning agriculture groups view Rollins as potentially promising, but still a wildcard on traditional agriculture policy. They were hoping for someone with extensive experience to help them counter Health and Human Services Secretary Kennedy's influence.

The long-term consequences of Trump's tariffs and ongoing plans for mass deportations will, in all likelihood, have a significant impact on the agriculture and food industries. These industries were responsible for a massive $1.58 trillion in the U.S. economy in 2024, and support more than 34 million American Jobs.

At her swearing in ceremony Rollins affirmed, *"It is... a privilege beyond description to have the trust of President Donald J. Trump, and the opportunity to advance his agenda. I am thrilled to lead the United States Department of Agriculture and to serve the people of this country,"* Rollins also said. *"Every day, I will fight for American farmers, ranchers, and the agriculture community. Together, we have an historic opportunity to revitalise rural America and to ensure that U.S. Agriculture remains the best in the world for generations to come."*

The question here is whether Trump's agenda and the revitalisation of U.S. agriculture are a compatible match and ultimately which one Rollins will choose to fight for.

Secretary of Commerce

Howard William Lutnick – July 14, 1961

Estimated net worth, March 2025 - $3 Billion

Lutnick has credited much of his private career success to his liberal arts education, but some struggle with how his liberal arts education could lead to supporting Donald Trump. *Clerk*, Lutnick's former College student newspaper, reported, Haverford College's Chair of Political Science Steve McGovern's opinion on Lutnick's support of Trump, *"...I do have a problem with a Haverford alum becoming a prominent backer of Trump... because his rhetoric and behavior are so offensive and hurtful to so many people, particularly vulnerable populations, and because Trump poses such a massive and unprecedented threat to basic democratic principles and practices"*.

Early Years

Howard Lutnick was the middle child of three children born in Jericho, New York to Jane (née Lieberman) Lutnick, a painter and sculptor and Dr. Solomon Lutnick a history professor at Queens College in New York. He was a senior in high school when he lost his mother Jane to lymphoma. His father passed away the next year, during Lutnick's first week at Haverford college. His father had been receiving treatment for colon and lung cancer and was accidentally administered an overdose of chemotherapy medication.

On hearing about Lutnick's fathers passing the President of Haverford College, Robert B. Stevens, contacted Lutnick and offered him a full scholarship for his four years at the college. This was a lifeline for Lutnick, and he graduated with a degree in economics in 1983.

Lutnick never forgot this generosity and since his graduation from Haverford he has become the most generous donor in school history, donating more than $65 million to the College. He also served as the Chair of the Board of Managers and funded The Allison and Howard J. Lutnick Library at Haverford College.

After graduating, he joined the financial services giant Cantor Fitzgerald, developing a long-term friendship with its co-founder Bernard Cantor. Cantor, who personally mentored Lutnick in his early career, recognised his exceptional financial talent and saw some of himself in Lutnick. Lutnick married in 1994 and he and his wife Allison Lutnick, a former Legal Aid lawyer, have 4 children together.

When Lutnick was only 29 he was named second in command of Cantor Fitzgerald, a year later he became CEO, and then chairman in 1996 aged just 35. Lutnick was one of the early players who understood the high value technology could bring to the financial services industry, and in 1999 he was fundamental in taking eSpeed, an electronic trading subsidiary of Cantor Fitzgerald, public.

Then in 2001 the world changed. Two planes struck the World Trade Centre in New York which housed the Cantor Fitzgerald offices and all of its approximately 1000 employees. Lutnick, like many other people in New York that day, made what would come to be a fateful decision. He took his eldest boy to his first day of kindergarten and so was not in the offices when the first plane hit. On hearing about the terrorist attacks Lutnick rushed back to the offices to find out for himself the scope of the devastation. After rushing to the North Tower Lutnick was forced to take cover under a car as the South Tower fell, possibly evading death a second time. Lutnick not only lost 658 employees that day, but he also lost his brother Gary and his best friend Doug.

In 2004, a decision was made between Lutnick and then head of the London office, Lee M. Amaitis, to split Cantor Fitzgerald into two separate operations. Lutnick continued on as chairman of Cantor, New York, oversaw a number of high-profile mergers, and founded his new standalone firm BGC Partners. He also held the position of executive chairman of the commercial real estate services firm Newmark Group, and launched the FMX Futures Exchange in 2024, a platform owned by some of Wall Street's leading investment banks and firms. Lutnick is no longer directly involved in the operations of FMX and stepped down from BGC Partners and the Newmark Group in February 2025 to take on the position of Secretary of Commerce.

Political Ascension

Lutnick and Trump have a friendship that spans several decades dating back to the World Trade Centre tragedy. In 2001 Trump was running the Trump Organisation's Real Estate arm in New York and aided Lutnick's firm with office space after the World Trade Centre terrorist attacks. They would often cross paths in the New York social scene with Lutnick making an appearance on Trump's reality TV show The Apprentice, in 2008. Lutnick has been a political ally of Trump since 2020, as a major donor to Trump's second presidential campaign and the host of high-profile fundraisers at his Hamptons property. He donated nearly $9 million to a Trump 2024 PAC and in October 2024, in a media triumph for Lutnick, *The Wall Street Journal* called him Trump's "top emissary to Wall Street."

In his abrupt New York fashion, Lutnick rose to the highest ranks of the Republican Party by outmuscling and outspending longtime Trump loyalists. It would seem Lutnick's tactics had worked as he secured the position of co-chair, with Education Secretary nominee Linda McMahon, of Trump's 2024 presidential transition effort, tasked with overseeing personnel selections.

However, following Lutnick securing the Secretary of Commerce position in February 2025, concerns were almost at once raised amongst U.S. trading partners, given Lutnick had been an impassioned advocate of Trump's tariff ideology. The trading partners felt the tariffs were simply being initiated to generate revenue for the U.S. Treasury and as a way to ensure compliance with the U.S.'s economic agenda. By April 2025, the impact of these well-founded concerns was being played out in the volatile global trading markets.

The Joker or the Riddler?

The role of the Secretary of Commerce includes promotion of National and foreign commerce and national economic growth, job creation, improved living conditions, technological competitiveness, and sustainable development. The Department of Commerce includes the offices of the Economic Development Administration, the Patent and Trademark Office, Bureau of the Census, and the National Oceanic and Atmospheric Administration Commissioned Corps.

Lutnick is admired as a man of enormous talent, a Wall Street innovator, and as being tremendously farsighted about financial markets. But it would seem Lutnick has swung both ways in his political affiliations or maybe he was just hedging his bets?

In 2016 Lutnick supported presidential Democratic nominee Hillary Clinton by hosting a fundraiser for her at his Upper East Side brownstone property. In the run-up to the 2016 presidential election, he made various contributions to the U.S. Senate campaigns of Democrats Kamala Harris and Charles Schumer and Republican Jeb Bush. But by 2020 Lutnick, it appeared, had pledged his allegiance to Trump and in 2024, in a display of his ongoing loyalty, Lutnick hosted a fundraiser at his Bridgehampton mansion, raising $15 million for Trump's campaign.

Trump choosing Lutnick was based upon several factors including Lutnick's long and immensely successful private sector career that makes him a credible addition to Trump's trade and economic team. Trump and Lutnick are longtime colleagues, who move in the same well-connected circles. Lutnick is highly regarded on Wall Street, stinking rich, and a financial mastermind willing to do what it takes to succeed. The bonus was Lutnick was yet another Trump convert. He may have only moved from fence sitter to full on Republican supporter but that doesn't matter to Trump, as in his mind, he won by flipping another opponent.

But Lutnick is said to have had dreams of becoming the treasury secretary. There is some speculation that the current secretary Scott Bessent wants out. To some the thought of the ingratiating Lutnick becoming Trump's emissary to Wall Street seems absurd. But given the disorganised chaos of the tariff fiasco, the fallout from the stock market's response and Trump's questionable cognisance, anything is possible. Maybe Trump gave Lutnick the consolation prize of Commerce Secretary instead of Treasury Secretary just to keep him in check, that though is anyone's guess.

Howard Lutnick came to symbolise much about New York and the events of September 11, 2001. He began the day as a quintessential Wall Street power player, wildly successful, famously relentless, and reportedly worth up to half a billion dollars. Just two days later, he was a shaken survivor, grieving the loss of countless colleagues and narrowly escaping death himself. But by September 15, public opinion had shifted dramatically, painting him as a cold-hearted villain for halting the pay checks of the deceased.

Then, on October 10, he introduced a generous and well-thought-out financial plan to support victims' families. Still, by that time, public perception had become murky, people weren't sure what to think of him. Ultimately, Lutnick was at least as charitable as other firms impacted by the attacks, sometimes even more so. But that early misstep on September 15 left a lasting dark shadow on his reputation. However, it has been said, in hushed tones, the Trump administration is where reputations go to die.

Lutnick is no man's fool, he just plays one. A constantly grinning joker-like character while on TV and in the Oval Office, a role played to please the leader of the free world, and a riddle of contradictions in his actions. Does Lutnick have a different agenda? He assured that Musk would not work in the Trump administration but would merely provide software for the government and he emphatically denied that Robert F. Kennedy Jr. would lead the Department of Health and

Human Services. Lutnick also declared that Trump intended to eliminate taxes for anyone making less than $150,000 and leaked information of a plan to privatise the U.S. Postal Service, resulting in a White House meltdown and threats of legal challenges.

These mistakes or missteps are not what would be expected of a seasoned financial services veteran. Could it simply be hubris, or is it something more?

Some thoughts:

On TV and in the Oval Office, Lutnick grins like a joker, an entertainer for the most powerful man in the world. But beneath the laugh lies a mind that moves markets. He knows the global reach of Trump's political theatre. He sees the numbered pieces before the rest of the world even knows there's a game. So why the mistakes?

Why publicly shut the door on Musk playing a role in the administration? Why draw a red line through RFK Jr.'s name, as if it was never pencilled in? Why declare a sweeping tax cut and leak the plan to privatise the Postal Service; moves that sent the White House into chaos, and cracked the image of control?

These aren't rookie errors. Lutnick didn't get to where he is by being sloppy with messaging, especially not when the stakes are this high. These moves destabilised

Trump's narrative, undermined internal coherence, and raised more questions than answers.

Is it hubris? The classic downfall, believing you're untouchable, that you can reshape the story with a smirk and a soundbite? Or is it something deeper, an alternative agenda? A quiet coup, maybe not to seize the crown, but to *remove* it. Perhaps Lutnick has come to fully comprehend the full arc of Trump's influence, the volatility, the chaos, the gravitational pull and understands the long-term cost of letting it run unchecked.

Maybe these aren't blunders at all, but pressure points, subtle destabilisers meant to weaken the foundation from within. So, if he's not trying to *become* the 'king' is he simply trying to make sure the kingdom doesn't fall into absolute ruin by slowing down its momentum? And if that means playing the fool on camera while engineering disruption behind a grin, so be it.

Secretary of Labour

Lori Michelle Chavez-De Remer – April 7th, 1968

Estimated net worth, October 2024 - $14.8 Million

In a meeting seeking the political endorsement of the Oregon Teamsters*, Lori Chavez-DeRemer brought her father, a long-time loyal member of the union, as support. In her endorsement request speech, she spoke passionately about her familial ties to the Teamsters and the U.S. labour movement. Her pitch was successful.

Many U.S. workers voted for Trump's MAGA rhetoric with sixty per cent of Teamster's members wanting the union to endorse Trump in 2024. They expected the Republican Party to follow through on its promises.

(*Teamsters, America's largest, most diverse union body with approximately 1.3 million members)

Early Years

Chavez-De Remer's grandmother legally immigrated to the U.S. from Mexico seeking the American dream. Chavez-De Remer was born in Santa Clara County, California, and graduated from the local Hanford High School in 1986. Raised by her father Richard Chavez, a Mexican American Teamster member who worked at a Safeway milk plant, Chavez-De Remer's understanding of labour issues are said to have been shaped by these early years.

She was the first in her family to graduate from college earning her Bachelor of Business Administration degree from the California State University, Fresno, California in 1990. She married her high school sweetheart in 1991, Shawn DeRemer an anaesthesiologist and investor, and they have twin daughters together. She worked in several distinct positions during the years between 1991 and 2004, supporting her husband while he completed his medical degree.

Chavez-De Remer's political journey began after her family moved to Oregon. She successfully gained a seat on the Happy Valley city council in 2004, became council president, and by 2010 was mayor, serving two terms until 2018. Her dedication and focus on local governance ignited her future political ambitions. She made two unsuccessful attempts for a seat on the Oregon House of Representatives in 2016 and 2018, both times losing to Democrat Janelle Bynum.

Political Ascension

During Chavez-De Remer's time as mayor of Happy Valley she had been invited to the White House, by the Trump administration, to discuss infrastructure development in her district. Her time in local government was instrumental in her being chosen as a delegate to the 2020 Republican National Convention as the representative for Oregon's Third Congressional District. Successfully running for a Senate position in 2022 she became the first Republican woman to represent the state of Oregon in Congress and was one of the first two Hispanic women to be elected from Oregon. During her time in the Senate, she served on several House committees in the areas of Agriculture, Education and the Workforce, and Transportation and Infrastructure.

Chavez-DeRemer only served one-term as a congresswoman. She lost the re-election in 2024 due to voters' concerns over her evolving perspective on labour policies. In her two years as a member of Congress she established a record championing workers' rights and organised labour issues that contradicted the Republican Party's traditional alliances with business interests. She had also been one of only a few House Republicans who backed labour reforms known as the *PRO Act*, legislation designed to help the unionisation of workers at a federal level. A stance that was questioned by several conservative Republicans during her confirmation hearing and one that appeared to threaten her successful confirmation.

(*PRO Act, Protecting the Right to Organise Act was proposed to give workers more advantages when organising or joining unions and workers bargaining with employers)

Chavez-DeRemer, however was free of politically volatile issues like the ones that plagued Trump's Labour nominees in his earlier term as president. Trump's first nomination as Labour Secretary, Andrew Puzder, stepped aside due to resurfaced allegations of spousal abuse, and his replacement, Alex Acosta, was forced to resign after being confirmed, due to his lenient handling of Jeffrey Epstein's case during his time as a federal prosecutor.

And on March 11, 2025, Chavez-DeRemer became the last of Trump's cabinet nominees to be confirmed.

Teamster or Trumpster?

Chavez-DeRemer, in her position as Secretary for Labour, will head a department that had approximately 16,000 full-time employees and an estimated $13.9 billion budget for the 2025 fiscal year. The Labor Department supervises a range of workplace laws, including wage, pay rules, child labour protections, federal safety standards, and safeguards for workers' retirement savings.

Trump has already rescinded a former President Lyndon B. Johnson-era executive order that required federal contractors to institute fair hiring practices. The Department of Labour's Office that monitors the Federal Contract Compliance Programs, is already considering slashing its employees by as much as 90%, as a consequence of the reduced workload resulting from Trump's directive. This is just one example of the efficiency actions instigated in the first weeks of Trump's second term. There has been a veritable tsunami of attacks on federal employees, labour-related agencies, immigrant workers, and jobs programs. Chavez-DeRemer's nomination, as a pro-union supporter of the *PRO Act*, for the labour secretary's position would appear to be in direct contradiction to Trump's political agenda.

Her tenure could go two ways, she could either transform the Republican Party's relationship with unions or be relegated to the back bench of the Cabinet. I personally don't foresee any major transformation happening within the Republican Party.

When Chavez-DeRemer was running for the open House District 51 in 2016, she was asked whether she would be endorsing Trump's 2016 presidential nomination, she said Trump, *"had not earned her endorsement."* Several years on from this opinion, in 2020, she posted on social media *"Over the past three years, President Trump exhibited strength in leadership and always put America first."* In the same year Chavez-DeRemer was named as a Trump Delegate to the Republican National Convention to support President Donald Trump's election.

After the 2024 loss of her Senate seat Chavez-DeRemer sought the Teamsters' endorsement for the Secretary of Labour position in Trump's 2025 cabinet. She won their support, by a single vote, and her long-standing union relationship started to pay off. Teamsters President, Sean O'Brien, organised a meeting with Republican lawmakers in November 2024 to pitch the idea of Chavez-DeRemer for labour secretary. She then flew with the Teamsters President to Trump's Palm Beach home for a formal interview. The Teamsters' endorsement had bolstered her status as the only union-backed Republican in Congress, even if it was by the thinnest of margins.

Chavez-DeRemer has shown she will toe the Republican party line and brings with her the support of one of the U.S.'s largest unions. She shifted her alliances to Trump, refused to disavow Trump's 2020 stolen election rhetoric, carries a Teamsters endorsement and has enough credibility in the labour arena to justify her position as Secretary of Labour. And she has no 'dirty laundry' to embarrass Trump's administration.

Trump's 2025 administration has already shown open hostility toward unions. An order to end collective bargaining by 50,000 airport screeners, an order to rip up union contracts and prohibit bargaining for over a million federal employees at many government agencies including the state department, the treasury, and health and human services. Tens of thousands of federal workers have been fired with a complete disregard for protections in their union contracts. Trump withdrew the $17.75 an hour minimum wage for federally contracted workers, issued an order to kill the Federal Mediation and Conciliation Service, and has repeatedly insulted the U.S.'s 2 million federal workers, saying: *"Many of them don't work at all,"* and *"Many of them never showed up to work."*

It remains to be seen what Chavez-DeRemer will be given the freedom to do in her role as Secretary of Labour in an administration with a dramatically anti-worker agenda.

Secretary of Health and Human Services

Robert Francis Kennedy Jr. – January 17, 1954

Estimated net worth, June 2023 - $15 Million

The many thoughts of Robert F Kennedy Jr. as reported by *NPR*, July 2023.

"Wi-Fi causes cancer and "leaky brain," Kennedy told podcaster Joe Rogan. *"Antidepressants are to blame for school shootings,"* he mused with Twitter CEO Elon Musk. *"Chemicals in the water supply could turn children transgender,"* he told right wing Canadian psychologist and podcaster Jordan Peterson, echoing a false assertion made by serial fabulist Alex Jones. *"AIDS may not be caused by HIV;"* he suggested multiple times.

Early Years

Born in Washington D.C., Robert F. Kennedy Jr. is the nephew of America's 35th President, John F. Kennedy, and the third of 11 children to Robert (Bobby) F. Kennedy, President Kennedy's brother and Attorney General, and Ethel Skakel Kennedy, a human rights advocate. Kennedy grew up with the trappings of wealth and influence that came from belonging to America's most iconic political family. He also experienced profound sorrow after the death of his father in 1968 and his uncle in 1963, who were both assassinated while holding political office. These events without doubt influenced his childhood and left an enduring mark on his perspective of the world and his chosen career and life path.

Not long after his father, Bobby Kennedy, was assassinated during his campaign for the 1968 Democratic presidential nomination, Kennedy struggled with drug addiction. Only 15 when he started taking drugs, his addiction would last for 14 years; the same addiction claimed the life of his brother David.

After being thrown out of two boarding schools Kennedy eventually went on to graduate from Harvard University in 1976, briefly studied at the London School of Economics before going on to receive his law degree from the University of Virginia Law School in 1982. He completed a post graduate master's degree at the Pace University School of Law in 1987 where he would later lecture on environmental law and hold the position of co-director of the Pace Environmental Litigation Clinic.

His legal career had a bumpy start when in 1982 Manhattan District Attorney Robert Morgenthau hired Kennedy as an assistant district attorney. Kennedy passed the New York State bar exam in 1983 but in February 1984, pleaded guilty to the felony charge of heroin possession. He was sentenced to two years' probation from practicing law and was required to complete community service. To satisfy the conditions of his sentence, Kennedy worked as a full-time volunteer for the Natural Resources Defence Council (NRDC), a nonprofit environmental group, and attended drug-rehabilitation sessions

Founder of the environmental group NRDC, Robert Boyle, mentored Kennedy and the mixture of the group's prior legal victories and Kennedy's iconic name helped them reach new heights in advocacy. Kennedy went on to complete the program for drug addiction and says he has been free of drugs since this time. He was also readmitted to the New York state bar in 1985.

After being readmitted to the bar Kennedy was appointed as a senior attorney for 'Riverkeeper,'* where he litigated and oversaw environmental lawsuits. There were many lawsuits filed against municipalities and industries based along the Hudson River, New York to stop discharging industrial waste and to enforce clean up measures from historical pollution. Environmental advocacy became the foundation of Kennedy's personal fame and achievement and in 1999, *Time Magazine* named him one of its "Heroes for the Planet" as part of a series on leading environmentalists. After many years Kennedy resigned from Riverkeeper in 2017.

(*Riverkeeper is a non-profit environmental organisation dedicated to the protection of the Hudson River and its tributaries)

Kennedy's descent into the realms of alternate theories became clear when during the 2004 presidential election he began openly promoting vaccine conspiracy theories. His theories hinged on a preservative that was used prior to modern vaccine formulas and its unsubstantiated connection to the rise in autism diagnoses. In 2005 he authored an article, considered the seminal piece that showed him as a major spreader of vaccine scepticism, where he made claims of a conspiracy involving mercury-based preservatives in childhood vaccines. This was a completely unproven claim and the preservatives in question had previously been removed from use, as a cautionary measure only, in 2001. Several corrections were made to the online article, and it was fully retracted in 2011.

He further claimed the government was complicit in allowing the pharmaceutical industry to use these preservatives and was therefore responsible for a generation of children being poisoned. During the COVID-19 pandemic he accused chief medical advisor to the president, Dr. Anthony Fauci, and philanthropist Bill Gates of spreading excessive fear to promote vaccine use, promoted Ivermectin* as a treatment for COVID, and later said the 5G cellular network allows governments to collect user data and to control citizens.

(*Ivermectin is widely used veterinary drug for treating and preventing parasitic infections in animals i.e.: heartworm in dogs and cats, and gastrointestinal and lungworm issues in livestock. It is also used to treat river blindness, intestinal infection from threadworms, and other kinds of worm infections in people).

Kennedy married Emily Ruth Black in 1982, a fellow University of Virginia law student. They had 2 children, but the marriage ended in divorce in 1994. He went on to marry Mary Kathleen Richardson Kennedy in 1994, an architect and philanthropist, and had 4 more children before Mary took her own life in 2012. Kennedy is currently married to actor Cheryl Hines who he married in 2014. Cheryl has one child from an earlier marriage.

Political Ascension

In 2023 Kennedy launched his campaign to pursue the Democratic presidential nomination, however many Kennedy family members publicly opposed him, instead endorsing Joe Biden. His reputation as a member of America's political royalty did not ensure his choice and after losing ground in the polls he dropped out of the Democratic primaries by late 2023 and entered the general election race as an independent.

Once Vice President Kamala Harris took over from President Biden, after he stepped down from the presidential race, it became clear to the Trump campaign that Kennedy could pose a greater threat to their voting numbers than Harris. Private talks were setup between the Trump and Kennedy camps with Kennedy expressing his willingness to endorse Trump if a deal could be made. The details of that deal may never be known but Kennedy did halt his independent presidential campaign in August 2024 and endorsed Trump's presidential candidacy.

It would be safe to say Kennedy's political manoeuvre assured him an influential position in Trump's administration.

A Cocktail of Conspiracy and Idiocrasy

The Secretary of Health and Human Services (HHS) advises the President on health, welfare, and income security plans, policies, and programs and is responsible for 13 operating divisions. These agencies are in place to oversee the financing of Medicare and Medicaid, conduct research with the aim to improve care quality, monitor health care fraud and abuse, and respond to pandemics. The secretary also oversees medical and scientific research and has broad power to distribute funding for the study of the causes, diagnosis, treatment, control and prevention of diseases. The HHS's estimated budget for 2025 was $1.8 trillion.

Well before COVID flipped the world on its head, Kennedy's reputation as an environmental lawyer had already been marred by his spruiking of conspiracy theories and activism against vaccines. But, during the pandemic he became the superspreader of COVID-related misinformation, gathering a loyal following specifically around that issue. Trump's spruiking of a populist and anti-intellectual worldview offers some explanation as to how a lifelong Democrat and nephew of a globally respected Democratic president, became a Cabinet member for a Republican president. The recognisability of Kennedy's name brought with it instant trust from huge swathes of the electorate, and Kennedy's anti-vaccine and conspiracy rhetoric appealed to voters who lacked trust in the political establishment.

Trump's choice of Kennedy as the Health and Human Services Secretary is yet another example of the "win at any cost"' mentality that is Trump's hallmark. Kennedy was chosen for his family's iconic name, his large fringe following, and his willingness to become yet another Trump convert. He is quite possibly one of the most underqualified and potentially disastrous choices Trump has made so far, and he's made a few.

The Health and Human Services website states that their, *"Departmental leaders are among the most qualified public servants in the Federal Government. They are dedicated to ensuring the guidance and management necessary to support the health and well-being of the nation."*

Robert F Kennedy Jr. was known as a crusading environmental lawyer who was instrumental in the clean up the Hudson River and who launched a global movement to protect waterways. Ironically it was his work fighting mercury pollution in waterways that led to his vaccine scepticism. He is said to have spoken to mothers who believed their children had been harmed by a mercury-based preservative in vaccines, moved by their stories he embraced the anti-vaccine cause.

(the mercury-based preservative had never used in the measles, mumps and rubella vaccines, which were the vaccines cited in concerns about autism).

Samoa's 2019 measles outbreak was a stark example of the terrifying impact of vaccine misinformation and fear mongering. More than 5,700 of the 200,000 people who lived on the island were infected with measles; 83 people died, most of those who died were young children. Just months before the outbreak Kennedy had visited the island nation as a representative of his Children's Health Defense non-profit. His rhetoric during his visit is believed, by Samoa's Ministry of Health, to have exacerbated vaccine hesitancy at a crucial moment, contributing to an atmosphere of mistrust.

Kennedy has repeatedly rejected the "anti-vax" characterisation, claiming he is not against safe vaccines and has vaccinated his children. He is the founder and chairman of the nonprofit organisation, Children's Health Defense, a leading promoter of vaccine scepticism.

Secretary of Housing and Urban Development

Eric Scott Turner – February 26, 1972

Estimated net worth, April 2025 - $2 Million

As Housing and Urban Development secretary, Scott Turner has oversight of billions in housing aid.

During his time as a Texas state legislator, he voted against protections for poor tenants and once called government assistance *"one of the most destructive things for the family."*

Early Years

Turner grew up in the Dallas suburb of Richardson, Texas and his parents divorced when he was eight years old. He graduated from J.J. Pearce High School in 1990, during this time he worked part-time as a dishwasher, and was a track and field star and cornerback on the school's Mustang football team.

His sporting skill enabled him to earn a full football and track scholarship at the University of Illinois where he gained a reputation for his defensive skills on the Fighting Illini football team. He graduated in 1994 with a Bachelor of Arts in Speech Communications. Turner and his wife Robin met when they both attended the University of Illinois. Marrying in 1995; they raised Turner's nephew Solomon, formerly adopting him when he was 8 years old.

His professional football career started in the National Football League (NFL) when he was drafted by the Washington Redskins in the seventh and final round of the 1995 NFL Draft. He played in the position of cornerback for the Washington Redskins for two years, moved to the San Diego Chargers in 1998 staying with this team until 2001, and played his final games with the Denver Broncos in 2003. Turner retired from the NFL in 2004 due to a leg injury.

Between 2007 and 2023 Turner worked for software company, Systemware, Inc. as their "chief inspiration officer" where he acted as a professional mentor, pastor, and councillor for the employees and executive team. He was an associate pastor at his local church, Prestonwood Baptist Church and is Chair of the Centre for Education Opportunity at the America First Policy Institute, a think tank set up by former Trump administration staffers.

Political Ascension

During NFL off seasons, he took on a position as an unpaid intern for then-Republican Senator Duncan L. Hunter, for California. After Turner retired from his NFL career in 2004, he accepted a full-time position working for the congressman. Turners first serious foray into politics was in 2006 when he ran unsuccessfully for a congressional seat as a Republican in California's 50th Congressional District. After this setback he moved back to Frisco, Texas where he was a motivational speaker and by 2012, he had successfully gained a seat in the state

House of Representatives. He was a member of the Texas House of Representatives for two terms from 2013 to 2017. Prior to finishing his second term Turner unsuccessfully challenged for the position of speaker of the house. He did not seek a third term.

During his tenure in the House of Representatives, Turner opposed many legislative government interventions for the housing market. He voted against the *H.B. 2473* legislation that supported foreclosure prevention programs, opposed legislation, *H.B. 1888*, that proposed to help public housing authorities replace or rehabilitate their properties, and sought to implement mandatory drug testing for poor families applying for government assistance. However, he did support some modest bills aimed at helping housing developments for seniors and those in rural areas seeking low-income housing tax credits.

Turner became the founding Executive Director of the White House Opportunity and Revitalization Council (WHORC) in April 2019. The WHORC was set up with the aim of supporting and promoting revitalisation in distressed and economically struggling communities, particularly through the use of "Opportunity Zones." Turner held this position throughout Trump's first term. He then started a nonprofit that promotes *"Christ-centered reading enhancement programs"* for children, took on the role of "chief visionary officer" with multifamily housing developer JPI and was a board member and Chair for the

Centre for Education Opportunity at the America First Policy Institute.

Turner was nominated in November 2024 for Secretary for Housing and Urban Development (HUD) and confirmed by the U.S. Senate on February 5, 2025.

Defender of the Poor or Anti-Poor?

The HUD's main responsibilities are to address the U.S.'s wide ranging housing needs, fair housing laws and housing for the poorest Americans. It is in charge of sheltering over 4.3 million low-income families via public housing, rental subsidies and voucher programs. The agency, has a budget of tens of billions of dollars, runs programs that do everything from reducing homelessness to the promotion of homeownership, funds construction of affordable housing and provides vouchers that allow low-income families to pay for housing in the private market.

It would first seem that Turner was chosen for the 2025 HUD position predominately due to his prior role as head of the White House Opportunity and Revitalisation Council. While this is partly correct, the former secretary of HUD, Dr. Ben Carson was Trump's first choice for this position, however he declined. Carson did, however, recommend Turner for the position, this endorsement turned out to be the deciding factor in his selection.

Turner is also a well-known and respected former NFL player who has wide public appeal and strong ties to the influential Christian lobby. Whether Turner has the relevant experience for this crucial role is another matter entirely. The U.S. is facing a substantial housing affordability crisis, clear in the shortage of homes, rising prices, and increasing costs for both renters and homeowners. The HUD's 2024 report showed an 18.1% increase in homelessness: 770,000 people were counted as homeless in 2024.

Is Turner the right man for the job? During his time in the House of Representatives he supported a bill that allowed the Texas legislature to support landlords refusing apartments to applicants because they received federal housing assistance. He also opposed amendments to a bill that would help expand affordable rental housing around "preservation area" housing.

Turner holds deep-seated scepticism about the merit of government efforts to alleviate poverty. He has called welfare dangerous and destructive to families and compared receiving government assistance to "bondage" and "like being kept in slavery."

Turner's views would seemingly place him at odds with the core work of the HUD. An agency that works to alleviate homelessness for millions of the nations marginalised, elderly and disabled. With an annual budget of some $72 billion, the agency provides rental aid to 2 million families, oversees the U.S.'s 800,000 public housing units, opposes housing discrimination and segregation and provides support to the nation's 770,000 homeless.

If Turner's record to date is any indication of how he will control the agency's agenda, it is those clinging desperately to the bottom of the housing market who have the most to lose. And then there's Trump's efficiency agenda to contend with.

Secretary of Transportation

Sean Patrick Duffy – October 3, 1971

Estimated net worth, April 2025 - $4 Million

Department of Transport regulators are investigating crashes involving Tesla's advanced driver-assistance systems and a crash reporting requirement that Tesla opposes. Safety advocates have voiced concerns that the Trump administration may move to end those investigations. Elon Musk was Trump's largest campaign donor and currently directs the Department of Government Efficiency (DOGE).

At Duffy's Senate confirmation hearing, questions were raised as to whether he would ensure traffic safety investigators would objectively follow the evidence as part of their ongoing investigations. Duffy assured the Senate that, *"Yes, I commit to this committee and to you that I will let NHTSA* do their investigation,"*

(*NHTSA - National Highway Traffic Safety Administration)

Early Years

Sean Patrick Duffy was born in Hayward, Sawyer County, Wisconsin, the tenth of 11 children of Carol Ann (née Yackel) Duffy and Thomas Walter Duffy. After finishing high school he gained a bachelor's degree in marketing from Saint Mary's University of Minnesota in 1994 and a Juris Doctor from the William Mitchell College of Law in 1999. Duffy, an accomplished lumberjack himself, managed a crew of lumberjacks and drove a 40-foot trailer of equipment throughout the country to show exhibitions as a way of paying his way through college.

In the late 1990's Duffy appeared in *MTV* Reality TV shows that highlighted Winnebago driving events, starring in "The Real World: Boston" and the "Road Rules: All Stars," where he met his future wife, Rachel. They later co-starred together on the "Real World/Road Rules Challenge: Battle of the Seasons," which aired in 2002.

Duffy and Rachel Campos-Duffy married in 1999. Rachel is known for her work as the host of *Fox Noticias* and co-host of *Fox & Friends Weekend*. They have 9 children together.

On graduating from law school, he practiced law in his hometown of Hayward as an associate attorney in a private practice, then as a special prosecutor at the Ashland County District Attorney's Office, before finally becoming the District Attorney of Ashland County in 2002. Transitioning into media he joined *CNN* as a political analyst, a role he held for nearly five years, while simultaneously, serving as the Financial Services practice co-head at the BGR Group. In January 2023, Duffy joined Fox Business team as a co-host on the *Fox Business* show, *The Bottom Line*.

Political Ascension

Wisconsin Governor Scott McCallum appointed Duffy to the position of Ashland County attorney general in 2002. He held the position for a further three terms until 2010. Duffy then stood for Congress and was successfully elected to Wisconsin's 7th District, going on to hold this position for ten years. He served on the House of Representatives Financial Services Committee and was active on local transportation issues via his co-chairmanship of the Great Lakes Task Force. Through his work with local law enforcement, he helped to make Ashland County one of the first in Wisconsin to investigate and prosecute child Internet sex crimes.

Duffy resigned from Congress in 2019 due to complications with his wife's 9th pregnancy and heart problems with their baby. He continued to contribute political analysis to *CNN* until 2020, held the position of senior counsel for the BGR Group until 2023 and was a political contributor to *Fox News* until 2024.

Trump nominated Duffy for the position of Secretary of Transport on November 18, 2024. He was officially appointed by the Senate on January 28, 2025.

Building Bridges or Burning Bridges?

The Department of Transportation (DOT) has a budget of more than $100 billion, plans and controls federal transportation projects and establishes safety standards for all major transportation types. The DOT employs almost 55,000 people right across the U.S., through the

Office of the Secretary of Transportation (OST) and its administrations and bureaus. Each of these bureaus have their own management and organisational structure, including the Federal Aviation Administration (FAA), National Highway Traffic Safety Administration (NHTSA) and the Pipeline and Hazardous Materials Safety Administration (PHMSA).

In 2015, Duffy was sceptical about then-presidential candidate Trump. In an interview on local radio station *WPR* he cast doubt on whether Trump could be trusted to advocate on behalf of the Republican voters if he did make it to the Whitehouse. Duffy, although he had in the past, did not endorse any Republican candidate in the 2016 presidential primaries.

However, Duffy's electorate overwhelmingly supported Trump in 2016 and in some areas, Trump led the vote by more than 25 points. By the time the mid-terms* came around Duffy recognised the need to rally his electorate to ensure Republican representatives maintained their seats. He orchestrated a campaign of Facebook ads supporting the Republican nominee in Wisconsin using the slogan, "There's Only One Candidate For Congress Who Will Support President Trump." These ads were very successful at reaching the voters and by May of 2018, with doubt about Trump dispelled, Duffy was inviting Facebook friends to sign Trump's birthday card.

(*Midterms; general elections held every two years, near the midpoint of president's 4 years in office. All house of representative seats and 33 or 34 seats of the Senate are up for election)

In 2019 Duffy introduced a bill, the *US Reciprocal Trade Act.*, designed to expand presidential powers to enable the imposition of reciprocal tariffs on foreign countries in line with existing tariffs on American goods. Even though Republicans in the Senate, who had previously sought legislation to limit Trump's tariff authorities disregarded the bill, Duffy earned high praise from Trump for his initiative.

Duffy has a reputation as a skilled and accomplished district attorney and 10 years' experience in the House of Representatives. In his time in Congress, he collaborated with bipartisan lawmakers to replace an 80-year-old bridge across the St. Croix River that spanned both his home state of Wisconsin and Minnesota. Although the bridge replacement was successful Duffy has relatively little other direct experience in the transportation arena or in leading a large organisation like the DOT.

Perhaps Trump sees a Kindred spirit in Duffy due to their both being stars on reality TV or it could be Duffy's loyalty and support shown toward Trump during his time at *Fox News*. But no doubt his "change of heart" played a part in his ultimate selection by Trump.

Duffy has already shown his loyalty to Trump as only hours after being sworn in as the new U.S. Secretary of

Transportation, he ordered the federal agency in charge of fuel economy standards to reverse standards that have been in place since the 1970s energy crisis. Since the onset of these standards cars have been produced that get significantly better mileage, effectively lowering the cost of driving for consumers and producing lower emissions into the environment. But this has also equated to lower sales for oil companies, both refineries and producers and goes directly against Trump's "drill, baby, drill" agenda for oil production.

According to the U.S. Environmental Protection Agency transportation was the largest contributor to U.S. greenhouse gas emissions in 2022.

Secretary of Energy

Christopher Allen Wright – January 15, 1965

Estimated net worth, November 2024 - $171 Million

Chris Wright, founder and CEO of Liberty Energy, has been one of the oil and gas industry's most outspoken critics of governments' efforts to fight climate change. He argues that increased fossil fuel production will raise people out of poverty and has stated that Trump's energy security plan will offer prosperity for all.

However, U.S. oil production is already at record highs and energy companies cannot be forced to drill for more oil. Further production increases could lower prices and reduce profits, not a palatable outlook for the oil and gas industry.

Early Years

Chris Wright was the youngest of four siblings, born in New Jersey and raised in Denver, Colorado. His father worked in the investment industry and his mother managed the home on a full-time basis. He gained his undergraduate Bachelor of Science degree in mechanical engineering at Massachusetts Institute of Technology (MIT) and completed his post graduate work in electrical engineering at the University of California, Berkeley and MIT. After graduate school, Wright secured a job in geothermal energy and in the late 1980's accepted a position with Hunter Geophysics whose main focus was technology for the oil and gas industry. In 1992, he founded Pinnacle Technologies, a company that developed technologies for mapping shale fractures. This technology was instrumental in helping to launch commercial shale gas production through hydraulic fracturing, or fracking. He was Pinnacle Technologies CEO until 2006.

In 2011 Wright founded and was chairman, and CEO of Liberty Resources LLC, a company formed to take advantage of the technology created at Pinnacle Technologies. In 2018 as the shale boom drove U.S. oil output to record highs, Wright took this company, now known as Liberty Energy, public and by 2023 the company was valued at $2.8 billion. He also holds board positions in the nuclear technology company Oklo Inc. and mineral royalty company EMX Royalty.

In a Liberty Energy report released in 2024 Wright wrote that he believes human-caused climate change is real, but that its hazards are *"distant and uncertain"* further saying, *"There is no climate crisis."*

USGCRP*, NASA*, and 97% of climate scientists worldwide disagree with Wright on this issue. They have found unequivocal scientific evidence that Earth is warming at an unprecedented rate, and human activity is the principal cause of the release of carbon dioxide through large-scale combustion of fossil fuels and widespread deforestation. The physical and socioeconomic impacts of extreme events are innumerable and are already being felt through increasing episodes and severity of droughts, wildfires, rising sea levels, and flooding.

Wright still lives in his home state of Colorado with his wife Elizabeth and family.

*(*USGCRP, United States Global Research Program. NASA, National Aeronautics and Space Administration)*

Political Ascension

Wright has no prior experience in government.

Wright is however close with billionaire oil and gas businessman Harold Hamm who has had Trump's ear on energy issues throughout Trump's first and second presidential terms. Hamm has been publicly vocal as to his preference for Wright for the Department of Energy position and had been promoting him for months prior to him being officially named for the position.

Hamm provided a platform for Wright to speak at an April 2024 dinner at Trump's Mar-a-Lago residence where top US oil executives had gathered for a fundraising event. This speaking opportunity catapulted Wright into top contention for Trump's cabinet.

Wright was confirmed by the Senate in a 59–38 vote on February 3, 2025, and was sworn in as Secretary of Energy later that same day.

Show me the Money

The Department of Energy (DOE) manages the U.S. nuclear weapons complex, nuclear energy waste disposal and 17 associated national labs, administers the nation's energy policy, runs grant and loan programs to advance energy technologies, and administers the Strategic Petroleum Reserve and had an estimated annual budget for 2025 of approximately $50 billion. The DOE has approximately 14,000 federal employees and over 90,000 management and varying contractor employees at the Department's headquarters in Washington, D.C., and at 85 field locations. The 17 national laboratories provide world-class scientific, technological, and engineering capabilities, including the operation of national scientific user facilities used by over 29,000 researchers from academia, government, and industry. It's not just about oil and gas.

Chris Wright, was a Republican campaign donor and has won support from influential conservatives, including oil and gas tycoon Harold Hamm. Hamm was instrumental in organising a fundraising event where Trump reportedly asked energy industry leaders and lobbyists to donate $1 billion to his presidential campaign, with the expectation that Trump would curtail environmental regulations and gut former President Joe Biden's climate agenda if he won back the White House. The American Petroleum Institute, an oil and gas industry lobbying group, released a statement in support of Wright's nomination saying his experience in the energy sector would provide the perspective that would guide his leadership.

It would appear Trump appointed Wright to enact his energy policies in an attempt to appease his industry supporters and to fulfill his "drill baby drill" political rhetoric. Although Wright undoubtedly has a long record of successfully managing oil and gas companies, the Energy Department is about much, much more than just administering oil and gas industry priorities and profit margins.

Nearly half of the DOE's budget in previous years was dedicated to maintaining and guarding the U.S.'s nuclear arsenal and several billion dollars was committed to efforts to combat nuclear terrorism around the world. Other areas that come under the DOE's banner are the administration of innovative alternate and efficient energy research low-interest loans, remediation of nuclear testing era sites, and the measurement of radiation levels at large public events in an effort to seek out possible terrorist bombs. The DOE has already felt the impact of Trump's cost cutting/efficiency spree with nearly 2,000 specialist trained staff fired. While these firings, once the impact of their loss became obvious, were mostly rescinded, this episode did not inspire faith in the Trump administration's understanding of such a critical and complex agency. This also brings into question, once again, their ability to appoint an appropriately experienced Secretary.

Wright will also serve alongside Secretary of the Interior Doug Burgum, who was also supported by billionaire Harold Hamm, on the newly formed 'National

Energy Council', which Trump states *"will oversee the path to U.S. energy dominance by cutting red tape, enhancing private sector investments across all sectors of the Economy, and by focusing on innovation over longstanding, but totally unnecessary, regulation."*

The U.S. oil industry is now suffering from the lowest crude oil prices in years due to Trump's tariff debacle; with prices falling dramatically in early April 2025. They are at their lowest since the COVID-19 pandemic, a drop that is testing oil executives' patience and has the industry rethinking its investments in new wells.

The probability of an economic downturn has increased markedly and slowing consumer demand for the industry's products may see their price plunge even further. It would appear Trump's trade policy fiasco risks destroying his plan for "energy dominance."

Secretary of Education

Linda Marie (née Edwards) McMahon – October 4, 1948

Estimated net worth March 2025 – $3.2 Billion

McMahon is overseeing an agency that President Trump has vowed to diminish. Dozens of Education Department employees were put on paid administrative leave with little to no explanation. Trump has called on Congress to close the department entirely and hand full responsibility back to the states with any programs not specifically protected by law to be shut down.

Early Years

Linda McMahon was born in New Bern, North Carolina and is the only child of Evelyn and Henry Edwards who both worked on the Marine Corps Air Station Cherry Point military base near their home. McMahon met her now estranged husband Vince McMahon, who is the son of a wrestling promoter, when they were teenagers. They married in 1966 after she graduated from high school. Three years later she graduated from East Carolina University with a degree in French. Though McMahon later earned a teaching certificate, she never actually taught, instead working as a receptionist and later as a paralegal. In 1976 the couple declared personal bankruptcy after accruing approximately $1 million in debt including five years of unpaid federal taxes amounting to $142,763.

However, by 1979, McMahon and her husband had made a deal with the owner of the Cape Cod Coliseum that essentially allowed them to pay nothing up front for the Coliseum while paying the mortgage payments using the profits made from events they ran there. They promoted both sports and wrestling events at the coliseum and in 1980 founded Titan Sports Inc. In 1982 McMahon and her husband bought the Capitol Wrestling Corporation from his father; these ventures would eventually become the World Wrestling Federation and later World Wrestling Entertainment (WWE). McMahon became president of the WWE in 1993 and CEO in 1997, ultimately leaving in 2009 to pursue politics.

McMahon and her husband have two children, Shane and Stephanie McMahon; both became involved with WWE and in 2024 Linda McMahon and her husband separated.

Political Ascension

McMahon gained an appointment on Connecticut's state school board in 2009, and in 2010 and 2012 ran for the U.S. Senate in Connecticut; she was unsuccessful on both occasions. Both of her campaigns for the Senate were predominately self-funded however one of McMahon's donors in the 2012 election cycle was Donald Trump, who contributed $5,000 to her candidacy.

During the 2016 presidential election, McMahon was a generous donor and supporter of Trump's campaign and after taking office in 2017 he nominated her to serve as administrator of the Small Business Administration (SBA). She held this position for two years before leaving to co-head America First Action, a super PAC backing Trump and the America First Policy LLC think tank where she later became chair of the board.

After Trump won a second term as president in 2024, he selected McMahon as his nominee for secretary of the Department of Education. During McMahon's Senate confirmation hearing in February 2025, she supported downsizing the department and Trump's policy of returning education to the states.

On March 3, 2025, McMahon was confirmed as Secretary of Education by the Senate, 51–45. She was sworn into the office later that day.

The Weaponised Dismantling of Education

The Secretary is the principal adviser to the President on federal policies, programs, and activities related to education and oversees the overall direction, supervision, and coordination of all activities of the Department. The department has a $228 billion budget and is responsible for the enforcement of many civil rights laws and ensures compliance with federal laws such as the, *Every Student Succeeds Act*.

Some of the Department's key responsibilities are administering funds to help school's low-income students obtain an equitable education; managing the *Individuals with Disabilities Education Act* that ensures services for students with disabilities; and overseeing the *Free Application for Federal Student Aid* (FAFSA) which helps millions of students afford college. FAFSA helps millions of students obtain Pell Grants, which don't have to be repaid, student loans, which do, as well as part-time work-study jobs.

In the U.S., education is mainly a state responsibility with each state having its own education system that appoints a significant amount of control to local authorities. The responsibility for setting many policies and approving budgets for their district falls on locally elected school boards. Federal funding accounts for approximately 14 percent of K-12 education, the states and localities fund the rest.

McMahon and her estranged husband have a history as confidantes and financial supporters of Trump's political goals. They supported Trump through his Trump foundation and were said to be one of the biggest donors, contributing $5 million in 2007. The McMahon's were also one of the largest donors in the 2016 presidential cycle, with a total of more than $10 million in donations.

Linda McMahon's limited education experience consists entirely of her appointment with the Connecticut State Board of Education in 2009, where she served for approximately a year. She may well be the least experienced and have the least amount of background in education of any previously nominated Secretaries of Education since the position was endorsed.

The Education Department is not a priority for Trump, as he has expressed on many occasions, and so McMahon's selection should be no surprise. Trump is intent on dismantling the federal agency and handing the responsibility back to the states and only requires a willing department head to assist him. He does however require an Act of Congress to succeed in shutting the department down completely, but that hurdle hasn't stopped him gutting the department in the name of efficiency.

Since Trump's administration took over in 2025 the Education Department has reportedly terminated all staff in six of the Office of Civil Rights' (OCR) 12 regional offices and has cut its workforce by nearly 50%. Gutting the OCR leaves millions of students without protections against discrimination based on race, colour, national origin, ancestry, sex, LGBTQ+ status, disability, and age. It reduces students' ability to seek justice and allows discriminatory practices.

The Education Department is also statutorily mandated to enforce national student privacy laws and to provide avenues to challenge abuses of their privacy. These protections are in place to stop the use of students and their family's information about things like grades, discipline, medical history and families' income. There are rising fears that information could be accessed by the

Trump administration's deportation division, ICE, for the purpose of tracking down alleged illegal citizens.

Secretary of Veterans Affairs

Douglas Allen Collins – August 16, 1966

Estimated net worth January 2018 - $0.45 Million

The Department of Government Efficiency (DOGE), overseen by "special government employee" Elon Musk, announced plans to eliminate more than 70,000 Veteran's Affairs (VA) workers. The savings from other ongoing cost cutting initiatives in the areas of software and consultants are said to be re-distributed to patient care. But there has been talks within the Trump administration of redirecting DOGE savings toward tax cuts or possibly dividend cheques. These redirections, if they proceed, are said to disproportionately benefit higher income earners.

Collins has stated he cannot guarantee that all the VA's savings will remain in the VA budget.

Early Years

Collins was born in Gainesville, Georgia where his father was a Georgia State Trooper, and his mother worked in aged care. After graduating from North Hill High School, he attended North Georgia College and State University where he gained a Bachelor of Arts in political science and criminal law in 1988. In 1996 he attended the New Orleans Baptist Theological Seminary, where he received his Master of Divinity. He was the senior pastor at the Chicopee Baptist Church in Gainesville for the eleven years from late 1994 to 2005.

After the September 11, 2001 attacks in New York, Collins joined the United States Air Force Reserve Command, serving as a chaplain from 2002 to 2012. During this time Collins also received his Juris Doctor from John Marshall Law School in Atlanta and in 2007 and set up his private legal practice. As a reserve member of the 94th Airlift Wing, Collin's was deployed to Balad (AL-Bakr) Air Base in Iraq for five months in 2008 during the Iraq War. He has served as a chaplain in the U.S. Air Force Reserve since 2002, reaching the rank of colonel in 2023.

Collins married his wife Lisa (née Jordan), an elementary school teacher, in 1988 and they have three children together: daughter Jordan and sons Copelan and Cameron.

Political Ascension

Collins served three terms in the Georgia House of Representatives from 2007 to 2013, winning both the primary and general elections unopposed. Shifting to national politics in 2012, Collins won Georgia's 9th Congressional District seat in the U.S. House of Representatives. He ran again for the U.S. Senate in 2020 but was unsuccessful. During his time in the House of Representatives he gained a reputation as a staunch conservative and a dedicated ally of Trump. Since leaving office in 2021, Collins served as Georgia's state chair for the Trump-affiliated America First Policy Institute and continued to advise Trump on legal issues, most notably on his efforts to overturn the 2020 election results. He also hosted "The Doug Collins Podcast" and is often seen on *Fox News* and *Newsmax* promoting conservative values.

Collins was confirmed as the Secretary of Veterans Affairs on February 4, 2025, by a vote of 77 to 23.

A Moral Duty; Veteran's Care

As VA secretary, Collin's is responsible for looking after the interests of more than 16 million veterans encompassing everything from education benefits, home loans, health care, funerals and disability compensation payments. The VA consists of three primary subsidiary organisations: the Veterans Health Administration (VHA), the Veterans Benefits Administration (VBA), and the National Cemetery Administration (NCA).

With an estimated 2025 budget of over $369 billion, the VA administers one of the largest integrated health care systems in the U.S., made up of more than 170 medical centres and over 1,000 other care sites.

The VA health care system has over 9.1 million enrolled Veterans and in 2025 is set to provide disability compensation benefits to nearly 6.9 million Veterans and their survivors and will administer pension benefits for over 224,000 Veterans and their survivors. The agency also administers the Loan Guarantee Service that has a portfolio of 4.0 million active home loans and manages the interment of an estimated 137,440 Veterans and their eligible family members in VA national cemeteries via the National Cemetery Administration.

During Collin's senate confirmation hearing he was questioned as to how he planned to solve difficulties regarding delivering timely health care, protecting whistle-blowers, and the perpetual quest to update the VA's electronic health record system, which has now spanned four presidencies. Collins vowed bipartisan cooperation.

Collins brings a mix of state and federal legislative experience and extensive military service to the VA role. The Senate Veterans' Affairs Committee advanced his nomination by an 18-1 vote and his 77 to 23 Senate confirmation vote reflects strong bipartisan support for his selection. Collins served as the ranking member of the House Judiciary Committee that defended Trump during his investigation by special counsel Robert Mueller into alleged Russian influence in Trump's 2016 election victory. That role and his book, *The Clock and the Calendar* gained him a nationwide reputation as a Trump devotee. Collin's book discussed Trump's first impeachment and allegations that he withheld military aid from Ukraine in a bid to force Ukraine into announcing an investigation into former President Joe Biden: arguing that Democrats were seeking revenge for Trump beating Hillary Clinton in 2016 and to prevent him from being re-elected in 2020.

Given his political experience, and military service Collin's was a popular bipartisan choice for the VA position. His dedicated backing of Trump's undertakings and agenda would also have been a factor in his consideration for the role.

Collins is the fifth member of Trump's 2020 impeachment defense team to be rewarded with coveted appointments. Trump supported Mike Johnson as Speaker of the House, John Ratcliffe as CIA director, Lee Zeldin as Environmental Protection Agency head, and Elise Stefanik as U.N. ambassador. Stefanik withdrew as a nominee for the U.N. position over fears her House of Representatives seat would be lost to a Democrat in the special elections. The Republicans only hold a slim majority in the House.

Secretary of Homeland Security

Kristi Lynn (née Arnold) Noem – November 30, 1971

Estimated net worth January 2025 - $1 Million

Noem was removed as a potential vice-presidential candidate after public outcry over an admission, in her book, *No Going Back*, that she shot a pet dog, a family goat and three horses. She said the stories were included to demonstrate she was prepared to do anything *"difficult, messy and ugly"*, in politics and in life. She also provoked anger after suggesting tribal leaders in her own state benefited from Latin American drug cartels. She was banned from seven tribal reservations, which covered one-fifth of South Dakota's territory.

The *Dakota Scout* uncovered blatant fabrications in Noem's book, *No Going Back*; she lied about cancelling a meeting with French President Emmanuel Macron and made-up a story about meeting North Korean dictator Kim Jong-un. A spokesperson for Noem, said that *"the publisher will be addressing conflated world leaders' names in the book before it is released."*

Early Years

Kristi Noem was born in Watertown, South Dakota to parents, Ron and Corrine Arnold, who were farmers and ranchers. While In 1994 while Noem was attending college at Northern State University in South Dakota her father died in an accident on the family farm. Noem postponed her studies and returned home to manage the family farm business with her brother. The family raised cattle and grew corn, soybeans, and wheat, and over time, as the business grew, they included a hunting lodge and restaurant.

Noem was an appointed member of South Dakota's Farm Service Agency committee, which implements programs and loans established by the U.S. Department of Agriculture (USDA). And in 2000, she testified before the House Committee on Agriculture in relation to the effects of USDA programs on family farms and ranches in South Dakota. This appointment was her first experience in public office and helped her pave the way to future representation opportunities.

She married Bryon Noem in 1992, and they have three adult children together, Kassidy, Kennedy, and Booker.

Political Ascension

During her campaigns she emphasised her experience in business, farming, and ranching, hoping to appeal to locals who could relate to her life and experiences. She also emphasised her prior work in state government where she had supported budgetary constraints, lower taxes and bills to increase gun rights. Noem was elected in 2006 as South Dakota's lone member to the U.S. House of Representatives, serving her first term in Congress between 2007 and 2010. She was then successfully re-elected, going on to serve as South Dakota's member of the House until 2019.

While serving in Congress, Noem took the opportunity to complete her education and took classes at South Dakota State University and the Watertown campus of Mount Marty College. In 2011, she graduated with a Bachelor of Arts degree in political science.

In 2013 Noem, after serving on the Natural Resources committee, joined the House Armed Services Committee where she worked toward protecting South Dakota's Ellsworth Air Force Base, an important contributor to South Dakota's economy. She was also instrumental in drafting legislation designed to protect members of the military from sexual assault and worked on a bipartisan proposal, with Representative Tammy Duckworth of Illinois, to extend maternity leave for women in the military. These provisions were successfully added to the *National Defense Authorisation Acts* passed in 2013 and 2014, respectively.

In 2018, after receiving Trump's endorsement, Noem was elected as the first woman to hold the position of Governor of South Dakota, and was only one of three Republican women governors in the U.S. She campaigned on a platform that emphasised protecting her constituents against tax increases, government growth, federal intrusion, and government secrecy.

However, Noem also built a reputation as one of the worst anti-LGBTQ+ politicians in the U.S. In a 2023 letter to South Dakota's Board of Regents, the group that supervises the state's higher education institutions,

Noem demanded they *"prohibit drag shows from taking place on university campuses"* and *"remove all references to preferred pronouns in all school materials and any enforcement of such."* While also paradoxically insisting that universities *"Remove any policy or procedure that <u>prohibits</u> students from exercising their right to free speech."*

Noem took over the position of South Dakota's 33rd Governor in 2019, was re-elected in 2022 with the largest vote total in the history of South Dakota and only resigned as Governor in January 2025 to take up the role of United States Secretary of Homeland Security.

Kristi Noem assumed office as secretary of homeland security on January 25, 2025.

Homeland Security: Difficult, Messy and Ugly

The Department of Homeland Security's (DHS) duties include, securing critical infrastructure, responding to natural disasters, prevention of terrorist attacks and protecting the president and other dignitaries. These responsibilities would ultimately fall to Noem who has practically no national security experience. Nevertheless Noem, will oversee the third largest Department of the U.S. government with a budget of $62 billion and a workforce of more than 260,000 spread across a copious number of complex and vital agencies.

The agencies that come under the DHS's mandate are the Transport Security Agency, Customs and Border Protection, Cyber Security and Infrastructure Security Agency, Immigration and Customs Enforcement, U.S.

Citizenship and Immigration Services, Federal Emergency Management Agency, the Coast Guard, Secret Service, Federal Law Enforcement Training Centers, and the Science and Technology Directorate. But the DHS issue that is most important to Trump is immigration. An issue that looks likely to be handled directly by the White House, through border czar Tom Homan, and deputy chief of staff for policy Stephen Miller.

Critics have argued that Noem, as governor of South Dakota a state with only 5% of the workforce of DHS and far from the immigration political hot spot of the U.S. southern border, lacks any expertise to run DHS. Noem's record of dealing with issues related to homeland security appears to consist of a speech given before the South Dakota Legislature that sought to foster fear about crossings at the U.S.-Mexico border. While Noem did authorise sending troops to Texas to assist in discouraging migrants, the deployment was fraught with ethical and legal irregularities.

Noem is pro-oil, anti-Obamacare, anti-abortion, and fervently opposed to the majority of the Obama administration's policies. She was a strong supporter of Trump in his first term, backing his Muslim ban and tax cuts for the wealthy. During the COVID-19 pandemic, Noem gained prominence within conservative groups for opposing government regulations designed to slow the spread of the virus: Trump praised her approach to pandemic restrictions. Since this time, she has become a regular presence in Trump's political world and in July 2020 she hosted Trump for a fireworks celebration at Mount Rushmore even though the Cheyenne River Sioux Tribe had previously opposed fireworks displays at a monument they view as a desecration of land stolen from them decades ago.

Noem's selection ensures an eager loyalist will head an agency that Trump sees as the cornerstone of his domestic agenda. She was one of the most vocal exponents of Trump's immigration policy during the 2024 election campaign, she has stated her willingness to do what is necessary to get the job done, and the mass deportation of 11 million undocumented immigrants does not phase her. Her selection for the DHS is an apparent reward for her loyalty. Noem openly supports Trump's vision of a nation that is blatantly hostile to immigrants and people of colour and along with other Trump cohorts is prepared to deny even legal pathways to immigration. They will do whatever it takes, no matter the financial or social costs, to bring about the most extreme and cruel deportation campaign in U.S. history.

Noem opportunistically positioned herself as a "defender of the border" even though South Dakota has no international borders. She dispatched the South Dakota National Guard to the Texas-Mexico border and made personal trips there while governor.

Texas Governor Greg Abbott came into conflict with the U.S. federal government (Biden era), after a scandal erupted when migrants were killed, after being caught in razor wire, while desperately trying to cross the Rio Grande river. Abbott had ordered the razor wire be specifically placed there. Noem, showed her support for Abbott by stating she would *"drive him more razor wire from South Dakota, if I have to, for him to do his job."*

Noem has said she was called to politics by God. *"the values I hold according to biblical principles impact my decisions: we are called to love, but we're also instructed to stand for truth,"* and *"In South Dakota today, we're just so grateful that every life is precious, and it's being recognized in this country."* It would appear this doesn't include immigrant or people of colour's lives.

MISC. OTHER KEY CABINET POSITIONS

Director of National Intelligence

Tulsi Gabbard – April 12, 1981

Estimated new worth January 2025 - $55 to $127 Million

Twitter post by Tulsi Gabbard, November 22, 2018, in response to the U.S. government standing with Saudi Arabia. There had not been any CIA assessment done of Saudi Crown Prince Mohammed bin Salman's involvement in the murder of *Washington Post* columnist Jamal Khashoggi in the Saudi consulate.

The Saudis' version of events shifted repeatedly after the journalist's disappearance from the consulate.

"Hey @realdonaldtrump: being Saudi Arabia's bitch is not 'America First.'"

Trump told reporters that Khashoggi's murder was a *"shame,"* but *"it is what it is…We're not going to give up hundreds of billions of dollars,"* said Trump in reference to an arms deal with the Saudis.

Early Years

Politics ran in Gabbard's family as her Catholic father Michael Gabbard was a state senator and her Hindu mother Carol (née Porter) held a position on the Hawaiian Board of Education. Gabbard, the fourth of five children, was born in Leloaloa, on American Samoa's main island of Tutuila. Her family moved back to Hawaii, where they had lived prior to her birth, when she was two years. Other than two years spent at a girl's school in the Philippines Gabbard was home schooled.

In 2003, Gabbard enlisted in Hawaii Army National Guard and by mid-2004 was deployed for a tour in Iraq where she served as a specialist with the Medical Company, 29th Support Battalion of the Hawaii Army National Guard. After completing her tour in 2005 she received a Combat Medical Badge for, "participation in combat operations under enemy hostile fire in support of Operation Iraqi Freedom III," and was later awarded the Meritorious Service Medal from the United States.

Prior to her deployment in 2002, Gabbard had married Eduardo Tamayo, but in 2006, citing *"the stresses war places on military spouses and families"* they divorced.

By 2007, she had graduated, top of her class, from the Accelerated Officer Candidate School at the Alabama Military Academy. The first woman ever to achieve this. Gabbard was then commissioned as a second lieutenant, appointed to the role of Army Military Police officer and assigned to the 29th Infantry Brigade Special Troops Battalion. She became one of the first women to enter a Kuwaiti military facility when she was stationed in Kuwait from 2008 to 2009 as an Army Military Police platoon leader. She also received the honour of being the first woman to receive an award of appreciation from the Kuwait National Guard.

Gabbard graduated from Hawaii Pacific University with a Bachelor of Science in Business Administration, in

2009, after her return home from her second deployment to the Middle East. In 2015, Gabbard married freelance cinematographer and editor Abraham Williams. Gabbard has spoken about their efforts to start a family and her unsuccessful in-vitro fertilisation (IVF) procedures.

In late 2015, she was promoted from the rank of captain to major continuing to serve as a Hawaii Army National Guard major until her transfer to the California-based U.S. Army Reserve unit in June 2020. By mid-2021 Gabbard had been promoted to the rank of lieutenant colonel while on deployment to the Horn of Africa where she was serving as a civil affairs officer in support of a special operations mission. As a lieutenant colonel, Gabbard has top-secret security clearance.

Political Ascension

Gabbard began her early political career as an aide to her father, Mike Gabbard's, right-wing populist political campaign that opposed equal rights for LGBTQ+ people. The group, The Alliance for Traditional Marriage and Values, was an anti-gay marriage political action committee. She also worked for Stand Up For America (SUFA), another right-wing group, founded by her father in the wake of the September 11, 2001, Twin-Towers attacks. Her father went on to become a national leader with his group, Stop Promoting Homosexuality, whose aim was to spread fear of "the Gay Agenda."

After dropping out of Leeward Community College, to run for election to the Hawaii State Legislature in 2002,

Gabbard became the youngest legislator ever elected in Hawaii's history. She was, at that time, the youngest woman ever elected to a U.S. state legislature and held the position until 2004. During her tenure in the legislature she enlisted in the Hawaii Army National Guard and in 2004 was deployed to the Middle East, rendering her unable to run for re-election.

After returning from her second Middle Eastern deployment Gabbard campaigned and won a seat on the Honolulu City Council. Turning her focus to gaining a seat in Congress, she resigned from the City Council in 2012 to focus on her congressional campaign.

Gabbard declared her candidacy for the Democratic open House seat of Hawaii's 2nd Congressional District in May 2011. After discarding her previous anti-gay rights rhetoric from her campaign, she won the nomination and was invited to speak at the 2012 Democratic National Convention. Gabbard became the first voting Samoan American and first Hindu member of Congress after defeating the Republican candidate. Her adoption of progressive politics helped her defeat her Republican opponents in 2014, 2016, and 2018.

Gabbard successfully introduced progressive legislation while in Congress. The *Helping Heroes Fly Act*, which expedited airport security screening for severely wounded veterans, received bipartisan support and passed unanimously in both chambers of Congress. Further in November 2015, she introduced legislation aimed at preventing child abuse and neglect on military bases called *Talia's Law*. Congress passed the legislation, signing it into law in December 2016. And, in 2018, she successfully passed an amendment to improve protective equipment for civil defence agencies that work near volcanic activity.

In February 2019, Gabbard became the first female combat veteran to run for president when she officially launched her 2020 presidential campaign and confirmed she would not be seeking re-election to her seat in Congress in 2020. While campaigning Gabbard missed a majority of votes in the House but did cast a "present" vote on both articles of impeachment in the first impeachment of Donald Trump. Some political figures felt her time spent on her campaign interfered with her Congress responsibilities. However, after suspending her presidential campaign in March 2020, she did resume regular attendance in the House.

Gabbard served on multiple committees during her time in Congress, focusing on military, foreign affairs, and financial issues and was a long-time member of the House Armed Services Committee, which focused on defence funding, military readiness, and intelligence oversight.

Defending the Homeland and U.S. Interests Abroad

The Director of National Intelligence is the head of the Intelligence Community, overseeing and directing the implementation of the National Intelligence Program budget and serving as the principal advisor to the President, the National Security Council, and the Homeland Security Council for intelligence matters related to national security. The Office of the Director of National Intelligence is a coalition of 18 agencies and organisations including the CIA and FBI that together employ more than 70,000 people. The Office was created to address intelligence failures exposed by the September 11, 2001, attacks.

Gabbard was first introduced to Trump by his first term chief strategist Steve Bannon in 2016. Bannon arranged a meeting with the president-elect at Trump Tower in New York as he felt she could potentially fill a number of positions within Trump's 2016 administration. Bannon admired Gabbard as an Iraq War veteran with an independent streak. This meeting did not eventuate in Gabbard having a role in Trump's first administration but by October 11, 2022 Gabbard announced, via a Twitter post, she was leaving the Democratic party to become an Independent, *"I can no longer remain in today's Democratic Party... driven by cowardly wokeness... racializing every issue & stoke anti-white racism, actively work to undermine our God-given freedoms, are hostile to people of faith..., demonize the police & protect criminals at the expense of law-abiding Americans, believe in open borders, weaponize the national security state to go after political opponents, and above all, dragging us ever closer to nuclear war,"* Gabbard posted.

It would appear Gabbard returned home to the provocative right-wing populism of her youth as shortly after this announcement she endorsed and campaigned for several Trump supported 2022 midterm election Republican candidates, became a contributor to *Fox News* and started her own podcast: moves that took her directly into Trump's domain. Following entry into the 2024 Republican presidential primary Trump named Gabbard as one of his potential choices for his vice-presidential running mate. On August 26, 2024, during a National Guard Association gathering, Gabbard endorsed Trump's re-election bid. Within 24 hours she was named as an honorary co-chair of his presidential transition team, and while speaking at a Trump Rally, on October 22, 2024, she announced she was joining the Republican Party.

Gabbard's political standpoints, have swung from her early political years as a right-wing anti-gay, anti-trans view to a liberal stance in her time as a Democratic candidate in the 2020 presidential primaries and back again. It would appear, via her media contributions, her position on social issues now aligns with the Republican Party mindset, including abortion, gun control, and anti LGBTQ+.

Gabbard was an unconventional pick to oversee and coordinate the country's 18 intelligence agencies. Considering her past as a long-time Democratic representative, her comments that were perceived to align with *Russian sentiments, a meeting she held with now-deposed Syrian president Bashar Assad and her support for government intelligence leaker Edward Snowden*.

(*Russian media aired Gabbard's foreign policy views, however there was no evidence of collaboration with Russian intelligence).

(*Snowden, a former National Security Agency contractor fled to Russia after being charged with revealing classified information about US surveillance programs. Gabbard acknowledged Snowden broke the law, but she also highlighted the exposure of illegal surveillance practices).

Gabbard, a military veteran with limited intelligence experience has been chosen to sit at the top of a pyramid overseeing the likes of the CIA, the FBI and the NSA. She did however, in her time in Congress, serve on the House Armed Services Committee, House Foreign Affairs Committee, and the Homeland Security Committee, and worked directly on issues involving national defense, intelligence oversight, and counterterrorism strategies. She participated in key hearings on emerging threats, such as cybersecurity and artificial intelligence in military operations. While she has no prior experience leading a government agency or department, her exemplary military experience and time in Congress were offered as qualifications for the role.

During her nomination hearing Gabbard asserted she would refocus on the office's core missions: coordinating federal intelligence work and serving as the president's chief intelligence adviser. Another loyal outspoken supporter of Trump, to "swap sides,'" no doubt added to her appeal for Trump.

Her military history and understanding of ethical behaviour offers some hope that Gabbard would, if push came to shove, look at the principles of the role she has taken on and stand against blatant corruption or ineptitude in the intelligence community.

Jeffrey Goldberg, editor-in-chief for The *Atlantic magazine*, March 24, 2025. *"The world found out shortly before 2 p.m. eastern time on March 15 that the United States was bombing Houthi targets across Yemen." "I, however, knew two hours before the first bombs exploded that the attack might be coming. The reason I knew this is that Pete Hegseth, the secretary of defense, had texted me the war plan at 11:44 a.m. The plan included precise information about weapons packages, targets, and timing,"* Goldberg wrote.

This Signal group chat involved 19 people including Defense Secretary Pete Hegseth, Director of National Intelligence Tulsi Gabbard, who was overseas and using her personal cellphone, now former National Security Adviser Mike Walz, CIA Director John Ratcliffe, and presidential envoy, Steve Witkoff, who was in Moscow at the time.

Just over a month later, on April 24, 2025, Tulsi Gabbard posted on X, *"Politicization of our intelligence and leaking classified information puts our nation's security at risk and must end. Those who leak classified information will be found and held accountable to the fullest extent of the law. Today, I referred two intelligence community LEAKS to the Department of Justice for criminal referral, with a third criminal referral on its way, which includes the recent illegal leak to the Washington Post. These deep-state criminals leaked classified information for partisan political purposes to undermine POTUS' agenda. I look forward to working with @TheJusticeDept and @FBI to investigate, terminate and prosecute these criminals."* This post was in reference to leaks in the intelligence community, not the Signal chat.

Director of the Central Intelligence Agency

John Lee Ratcliffe – October 20, 1965

Estimated net worth – 2019 - $6.8 Million

Previous intelligence agency leaders have carried out their work in the shadowy confines of the CIA establishment. But CIA Director John Ratcliffe wants the world to know he is faithfully carrying out Trump's agenda.

Appearing on *Fox News*, as is par for the course, and reposting Trump's statements from social media, Ratcliffe has been curiously public in speaking about his efforts to align with Trump's ambitions.

Early Years

Ratcliffe was born in Chicago, Cook County, Illinois, the youngest of six children to parents who were both teachers. He graduated from Carbondale Community High School, Carbondale, Illinois, in 1983, going on to successfully earn a scholarship to the University of Notre Dame, Illinois where in 1987 he completed a Bachelor of Arts in government and international studies.

Ratcliffe successfully attained his Juris Doctor from Southern Methodist University School of Law, Dallas, Texas, in 1989, where he met his wife Michele: the couple have two daughters together.

After gaining his Juris Doctor he worked in private practice and in 2004 was elected to four consecutive two-year terms as mayor of Heath Texas, an unpaid and non-partisan position, serving until May 2012. During this time, he also held a position in the Texas Eastern Districts Attorney General's office. In 2009, Ratcliffe and former U.S. Attorney Johnny Sutton founded a law firm together in Texas. The firm, Ashcroft Sutton & Ratcliffe became part of the Ashcroft Group: a Washington D.C. lobbyist firm founded by former U.S. Attorney, under George W Bush, John Ashcroft.

At various times Ratcliffe has served as an Adjunct Professor of Law at various law schools, including Southern Methodist University and Texas Wesleyan University.

Political Ascension

Ratcliffe held a position within the Texas U.S. Department of Justice and in 2004 former President George W Bush appointed him as Chief of Anti-Terrorism and National Security for the Eastern District of Texas, a position he held until 2007. Ratcliffe then took over the role of acting U.S. Attorney for the Eastern District of Texas, until 2008.

Ratcliffe gained a Republican Senate seat in 2015 and served for more than five years as the U.S. Representative for the 4th Congressional District of Texas. He gained a reputation as a policymaker on national security issues as a member of the House Intelligence, Homeland Security, and Judiciary committees. He resigned from this position in May of 2020, to take on the role of Director of National Intelligence (DNI); a position he held until the end of Trump's first presidential term in January 2021. During his limited time as DNI Ratcliffe designated space a priority intelligence domain and included the U.S. Space Force as the 18th member of the U.S. National Intelligence Community.

After leaving the Trump administration in 2021, Ratcliffe was a visiting fellow at the Heritage Foundation where he was tasked with "helping Project 2025 build out policy recommendations for intelligence reform in the next presidential administration." Ratcliffe contributed to Project 2025, by providing information for a section of a chapter on the intelligence community and served as Co-Chair for the Center for American Security at the America First Policy Institute until 2024

Ratcliffe was officially sworn in as Director of the Central Intelligence Agency on January 23, 2025. He now holds the position of being the first person ever to serve as both Director of National Intelligence and as Director of the Central Intelligence Agency.

An Administrative Espionage Agent

As the Director of the CIA, Ratcliffe is responsible for managing the Agency's intelligence collection, analysis, covert action, counterintelligence, and liaison relationships with foreign services. He also oversees the management of foreign intelligence acquired by human sources, known as HUMINT. The budget and official number of employees are not publicly disclosed however it is estimated to have a budget of around $15 billion and approximately 21,000 employees. The Director of the CIA is required to report to the Director of National Intelligence, Tulsi Gabbard.

Ratcliffe has an extensive Senate and legal background and past experience as Director of National Intelligence, albeit for less than twelve months, in Trump's first term. That Trump would elevate Ratcliffe to this post is unsurprising. Ratcliffe is an unwavering Trump supporter who defended him through numerous investigations during his first term and was part of Trump's defence team during his first impeachment in 2020, offering advisory and television advocacy roles.

Given some of Trump's controversial picks for other roles, Ratcliffe is considered to be a more traditional choice given his prior history in the role and his time in the Senate.

Ratcliffe often boasted about his experience as a terrorism prosecutor and for years exaggerated his role in the "Holy Land" case as a way of bolstering his national security qualifications, suggesting that he was directly involved in bringing the alleged terrorists to justice. Ratcliffe's name cannot be found in any court documents related to the prosecution or any of the numerous media stories written about the investigation and trial.

In the one terrorism-related case he claims to have worked on, the Texas-based Muslim charity Holy Land Foundation for Relief and Development, he is reported as playing a minor part at best.

After the first "Holy Land" trial Ratcliffe, as the neighbouring Eastern U.S. attorney, was asked to lead an independent internal inquiry for the Northern District of Texas, as allegations had surfaced about possible inappropriate contact between a juror and Justice Department employees. According to others who worked on the case this was the scope of Ratcliffe's involvement.

Chief of Staff

Susie (née Summerall) Wiles – May 14, 1957

Estimated net worth - $10 Million

Even after Trump's loss of 2020 and the political and media fallout that followed; the January 6, insurrection of 2021, the Republican party's losses in the 2022 midterms, the numerous criminal indictments of 2023 and the ongoing trials of 2024, Trump still secured the 47th U.S. presidency in 2024. Trump's capacity to ignite his devoted followers cannot be denied but Susie Wiles has been heralded as being the driving force behind Trump's return from the ashes.

Early Years

Born and raised in Saddle River, New Jersey, Susie Wiles is one of three children of Pat Summerall and his wife Katherine (née Jacobs) Summerall. She was the only daughter and oldest of the three children, the child of an alcoholic father and a mother who worked desperately to keep order around him. From an early age she learnt to cope, as she saw her mother do, with courage and grace. Her father had endured a brutal childhood: A father he never knew, a stepfather who beat him with a rubber hose, and a mother who abandoned him as a toddler. Alcohol became a way of coping, for Wiles' father Pat; childhood trauma and its outcomes were not fully understood or dealt with in the 1950's. Wiles' family supported her father through rehabilitation, helping him beat his alcohol addiction. He played football in the National Football League and later in life, after retiring as a player, became a successful sportscaster, announcing a record 16 Super Bowls. This time in Wiles' life shaped the adult she became, she gained personal strength through her families struggles but also developed an intense desire to succeed and be invaluable to those she advocated for.

Wiles graduated from the Academy of Holy Angels High School in 1975 and went on to graduate from the University of Maryland, College Park with a Bachelor of Arts in English Language. She married Lanny Wiles, a Republican consultant and special assistant to former president Ronald Reagan, in 1985. They divorced in 2017 and have two children together.

Political Ascension

In 1979, Wiles was hired as an entry level staffer for Representative Jack Kemp, in part because of her father's friendship with Kemp, a former NFL teammate. She soon proved herself valuable and the next year, she took on a position as a campaign scheduler for Ronald Reagan's 1980 presidential campaign; she met her future husband Lanny wiles during this period.

In the 1990s Wiles worked as director of communications and intergovernmental affairs for then major of Jacksonville, John Delaney. She went on to be deputy chief of staff, ultimately becoming the first woman to hold the position of Jacksonville's chief of staff. Wiles also worked for Congresswoman Tillie Fowler as a district director.

She advised the mayor of Jacksonville, John Peyton from 2004 to 2009, as his chief of special initiatives and communications. And, in the 2010 Florida Gubernational* election, Wiles was credited with progressing Rick Scott, a then-businessman and Navy veteran with little political experience, into Florida's governor in just seven months. Rick Scott served two terms as governor and is now a U.S. senator representing Florida.

(*Gubernational election – the election of state and territory governors in the U.S.)

In January 2011, Wiles was hired as campaign manager for former governor of Utah Jon Huntsman Jr's presidential campaign. In mid-2011 she left the Huntsman campaign, when she and NFL player Tony Boselli, collaborated to lead the Ponte Vedra, Jacksonville lobbyist office of Smith & Ballard, now known as Ballard Partners. Wiles, a registered lobbyist, worked at the firm for eight years; leaving in 2019, because of a health issue, though she continued lobbying for clients through the firm until 2022.

In August 2015 Wiles went to New York to meet with Donald Trump at a Trump Tower meeting arranged by lobbyist Brian Ballard of Ballard Partners. This was to be the start of a remarkably interesting decade in Wiles' career.

Wiles ran Trump's campaign operations in Florida in the 2016 presidential election cycle and in 2018 Trump requested her help for Republican Ron DeSantis' campaign for governor. DeSantis won but in 2020 Wiles was removed from her role because DeSantis, his wife and his chief of staff thought she was getting too much credit for DeSantis' win. They accused her of working more for her own lobbyist clients and less for the governor's agenda. DeSantis forcefully pushed her out of his political operation and then maliciously urged Trump to do the same. Trump sided with DeSantis and removed Wiles from his re-election team. Trump soon regretted his choice.

Trump desperately needed to win the Florida seat to get re-elected and he needed Wiles to do for him, in 2020, what she had previously done for him in 2016. DeSantis' opinions were soon pushed aside. Wiles felt the need to prove herself after the DeSantis accusations; accepting the role she committed to win Florida for Trump. Florida turned out to be the only swing state Trump won in a federal election that he ultimately lost. In March 2021, Wiles was chosen as CEO of Trump's Save America PAC. Wiles also served as Co-Chair of giant lobby firm Mercury Public Affairs for their Miami and Washington, D.C., offices in 2021. As a registered lobbyist between November 2017 and April 2024, she was registered to lobby the U.S. federal government for 42 different clients, including large corporations, government contractors, and business associations. Wiles lobbied the White

House, Congress, and federal agencies about regulations, federal policy, and business development. Wiles' federal lobbying clients have included: a waste management company who has been fighting the removal of nuclear waste from its radioactive landfill, a copper and gold mining company seeking to dig a mine in an unspoiled watershed, and a tobacco company seeking to block health restrictions on its candy-flavoured cigars, which the Food and Drug Administration has found are attractive to children.

As history now attests, Wiles lead a triumphant 2024 presidential campaign, securing Trump a second term as president. Two days after Trump's victory Wiles was selected as his new White House chief of staff, the first woman in U.S. history to hold the role. Congressional confirmation is not required for this role.

Wiles told Trump she intended to instill order among his staff. Nevertheless, Trump nominated Matt Gaetz as his first choice for Attorney General when she was not present: that appointment did not end well (see Pam Bondi), and she is said to have been displeased at Elon Musk's interference with her staff.

Mutual Regard

The chief of staff is considered to be the president's top aide and plays a crucial role in every president's administration. Essentially the manager of the White House, Wiles is responsible for putting together the president's staff and overseeing all daily operations and staff activities. She also advises Trump on policy issues and directs and oversees policy development. Wiles is said to have requested more say and control in the day to day running of the White House, an issue that plagued Trump's Chief's of Staff in his previous term.

Wiles' primary qualification for handling Trump could arguably be traced back to her training handling her father. Her childhood gave her the skills to deal with unstable, dysfunctional, notable men. She knows when she can help, and she knows when to step back. Teaching herself to be invaluable, or invisible, whichever the moment called for.

Unlike other candidates Trump didn't simply choose Wiles, they chose each other. You may ask yourself why such a successful woman with the talent to deal with the cutthroat world of Washington would choose to take on such a role with a highly controversial president like Trump.

Wiles explained this as, *"And so, you just sort of take the good with the bad,"* Wiles said, *"with everybody."*

Wiles' sharp intelligence, mild demeaner, and level head causes confusion among liberals and anti-Trump conservatives. They believe she is smart enough and sane enough to know better than to support and advance a personality like Trump.

Liberals console themselves with platitudes like, *"At least **he**, they say, is listening to **her**"*.

However, some have come to see her as an accomplice to all that is happening and the ongoing terrible consequences of Trump's second term. They believe without a collaborator like Wiles; any would-be autocrat would be unable to get or wield such potentially destructive power.

Director of the Office of Management and Budget

Russell Thurlow Vought – March 26, 1976

Estimated net worth 2025 - $1 Million

Vought has described himself as a Christian nationalist who believes Christianity should have influence over the government and society. In private speeches for the lobby group, Center for Renewing America, he called January 6 rioters *"political prisoners"* and condemned what he called the *"transgender sewage that's being pumped into our schools and institutions."* Vought advocated for the defunding of selected federal agencies and demonised career civil servants, including scientists and subject matter experts.

"When they wake up in the morning, we want them to not want to go to work because they are increasingly viewed as the villains" Vought said, and *"we want their funding to be shut down so that the EPA can't do all of the rules against our energy industry..."*

"We want to put them in trauma."

Early Years

Vought was born in Washington and raised in Virginia. He was the youngest of six children, to parents Thurlow Bunyea Vought, an electrician and U.S. Marine Corps veteran, and Margaret Flowers (née Smith) Vought, an elementary school teacher. He earned a Bachelor of Arts in political science from Wheaton College, an evangelical Christian college in Illinois in 1998, and a Juris Doctor from the George Washington University Law School in 2004.

Other than a long political career, Vought served as vice president of Heritage Action for America for seven years, the lobbying arm of the Heritage Foundation.

Vought was formerly married to Mary Grace Vought, the President and Founder of Vought Strategies, a Washington D.C. based PR firm established in 2013, with whom he shares two daughters. Mary filed for divorce on August 4, 2023, and the divorce was quickly finalised on August 30, 2023.

Political Ascension

Vought's political career commenced on Capitol Hill, where he served as a Republican legislative assistant for U.S. Senator Phil Gramm between 1999 and 2002, Senator Chuck Hagel from 2002 to 2003, and Senator Jeb Hensarling between 2003 and 2004. In these roles, he honed his skills in legislative processes and policy formulation. He subsequently became the Executive Director of the Republican Study Committee from 2004 to 2009, where he played a role in shaping conservative legislative agendas and later as the Policy Director for the House Republican Conference, under then Chairman Mike Pence, between 2009 and 2010.

Vought held the position of vice president of Heritage Action for America for seven years, a sister organisation to the Heritage Foundation, which produced the now-infamous Project 2025. * Vought was one of the co-authors of Project 2025, writing a section on the Executive Office.

(*Project 2025 is a nationalist plan to dismantle the government, recruit thousands of politically aligned people to staff the administration, and guide President Trump toward their preferred 'conservative' policy changes).

In April 2017, Trump nominated Vought to be Deputy Director of the Office of Management and Budget (OMB). He was successfully confirmed by the Senate on February 28, 2018, in a 50–49 vote with Vice President Mike Pence cast the tie-breaking vote. In early 2019 serving OMB director Mick Mulvaney took on the role of acting White House Chief of Staff and Vought became the acting OMB director. In early 2020, Trump officially nominated Vought for the OMB Director's role. After being confirmed by the Senate he held the position until the end of Trump's first presidential term.

After Trump's first term ended Vought founded a charitable organisation called the Center for Renewing America (CRA). CRA and the affiliated issue advocacy group, American Restoration Action, focused on combating critical race theory. * The stated mission of the groups was to *"renew a consensus of America as a nation under God"* and *"provide ideological ammunition to sustain Trump's political movement after his departure from the White House."*

(*Critical Race Theory; a set of ideas that racial bias is inherent in many parts of western society, particularly in legal and social institutions, on the basis they were predominantly designed by and for white people).

On November 23, 2024, Trump announced he would nominate Vought as director of the OMB for his second term. The U.S. Senate voted 53–47 on February 6 to approve his nomination.

Upon taking office as OMB Director, Vought was also installed as acting director of the Consumer Financial Protection Bureau and Director of the Federal Insurance Corporation (FIC). The FIC was setup to preserve and promote public confidence in the U.S. financial system by underwriting deposits in banks and savings institutions for at least $250,000. Three enormously powerful economic roles within the government.

Unilateral Power to Trump

The OMB is the largest section of the Executive Office of the President, reports directly to the President, and helps to implement and enforce the commitments and priorities of the President.

The OMB has five critical processes it carries out; budget development and execution, management, coordination and review of all significant Federal regulations by executive agencies, legislative clearance and coordination of all agency communications with Congress, including testimony and draft bills, and reviews and clears draft Executive Orders and

Presidential Memoranda to agency heads and officials prior to their issuance.

Vought successfully ascended to the position of Director of the OMB in Trump's first term giving him specific history and experience in the role. However, he actively strove to decimate agency budgets and regulations, proposed severe cuts to Medicaid and the Department of Education, and worked to disenfranchise career civil servants during his tenure in Trump's first term.

Under the U.S. Constitution, budget bills must be passed by Congress and signed into law and decisions on how to spend U.S. taxpayer money, once this has occurred, cannot be unilaterally altered by the President. Vought's affiliation with Project 2025 calls into question his objectivity for this role as Project 2025 endorses an OMB that would oversee and enforce an overreach of presidential authority over budgets and congressionally authorised spending programs. In Project 2025, Vought writes, "*OMB can then direct on behalf of a President the amount, duration, and purpose of any apportioned funding to ensure against waste, fraud, and abuse and ensure consistency with the President's agenda and applicable laws.*"

Vought has previously demonstrated his contempt for and willingness to ignore Congress' power and the corresponding depth of his loyalty to Trump. He was one of nine government officials in 2019 who openly defied a subpoena to testify before Congress in relation to the Trump-Ukraine scandal and allegations relating to the Trump administration's decision to freeze military aid to Ukraine.

Any reasonable person would have expected Congress to reject a man who openly declares he will ignore both the Constitution and the Congress. As history now shows they didn't.

In 2020, Vought, at Trump's bidding, issued an OMB memo instructing federal agencies to cease all training on "critical race theory" or "white privilege". Any training effort that taught or suggested that either, the U.S. is an inherently racist or evil country or that any race or ethnicity is inherently racist, or evil was to cease. Agencies were also instructed to identify legal avenues to cancel contracts or otherwise divert the "millions of taxpayer dollars" being spent on such training. The OMB memo stated the training provoked division and resentment within the federal workforce.

Journalists from the U.K. *Centre for Climate Reporting* covertly recorded a meeting with Vought in 2024 where he asserted that elected leaders should discuss whether to prioritise Christian immigrants over those of 'other' religions.

Administrator of the Environmental Protection Agency

Lee Michael Zeldin – January 30, 1980

Estimated net worth 2024 - $1 to 5 Million

Nonprofit and state Government agencies including Habitat for Humanity, United Way, and the New York State Department of Taxation and Finance were charged with conspiracy to defraud the U.S. The funds, allocated by the previous Biden administration, had been received legally through the "Greenhouse Gas Reduction Fund."

As a result of these charges, brought by the EPA and the FBI, Citibank froze the accounts of these organisations without notice rendering them unable to access vital funds. This action was in Zeldin's first month of taking over the EPA. The Wall Street Journal reported Zeldin as saying, *"We are driving a dagger through the heart of climate-change religion and ushering in America's Golden Age."*

Early Years

Zeldin was born in East Meadow, Nassau County, New York the son of Merrill (née Schwartz) Zeldin and David Zeldin. Zeldin's parents divorced when he was in grade school and he was raised with a mix of Conservative Judaism and Reform Judaism. Raised in Suffolk County, New York Zeldin graduated from William Floyd High School in Mastic Beach, New

York, in 1998 and also attended Hebrew School. Zeldin received his Bachelor of Arts degree in political science from the SUNY University at Albany in 2001 and his Juris Doctor from Albany Law School in May 2003. In 2004, he was admitted to the New York State Bar and at the age of 23 became New York's youngest lawyer.

After receiving an Army ROTC commission as a second lieutenant in 2003, Zeldin served in the U.S. Army's 82nd Airborne Division in military intelligence and the legal corps, deploying to Iraq in 2006. In 2007, he transitioned from active duty to the Army Reserves, where he went on to achieve the rank of lieutenant colonel before finally retiring on April 30, 2025. In 2007 after leaving active duty, Zeldin took the position as attorney for the Port Authority of New York and New Jersey. In 2008, he and his wife Diana started their own general-practice law firm in Smithtown, New York which Zaldin practiced in full-time until he was elected to New York's 3rd State Senate district in 2010.

Zeldin's wife Diana works in a local law firm as a patent specialist, and the couple have identical twin daughters Mikayla and Arianna. They live in Shirley, New York and Zeldin is a member of B'nai Israel Reform Temple in Oakdale.

Political Ascension

In 2008, Zeldin unsuccessfully challenged Democratic incumbent Tim Bishop in New York's 1st district congressional elections. In 2010 he tried his luck in the

New York 3rd State Senate district and successfully defeated Democratic incumbent Brian Foley with 57% of the vote and went on to be re-elected in 2012 with 56% of the vote.

Zeldin again sought the federal Republican nomination for the House of Representatives Congressional seat in 2014. On his second attempt he successfully beat Democrat Tim Bishop, and retained this seat in the 2016, 2018, and 2020 election cycles. After finishing his four terms in Congress, Zeldin founded and chaired a charity called Zeldin Cares, joined the Board of the Republican Jewish Coalition, and founded consulting firm Zeldin Strategies. In April 2021, Zeldin announced his intention to run for governor of New York in the 2022 elections. During his campaign for governor Zeldin visited every county in New York State twice and in November 2021 declined to commit to campaigning with Trump, saying, *"There are plenty of New Yorkers who love him, there are plenty of New Yorkers out there who don't."* Although the election was close Zeldin lost to incumbent governor Kathy Hochul, 53.2% to 46.8%.

Zeldin has held memberships in several caucus' including the Conservative Climate Caucus*. Climate Solutions Caucus and was the Co-chair for the Long Island Sound Caucus. He also held two positions with the America first Policy Institute (AFPI); Chair of AFPI's Pathway to 2025 Initiative and Chair of their China Policy initiative.

(*Caucus is an informal organisation of members of the House or Senate that exist to discuss issues of mutual concern).

Zeldin was nominated as Administrator of the EPA as part of Trump's second administration in November 2024 and was confirmed by the Senate and sworn in on January 29, 2025.

'Climate Change is Real'

The EPA is responsible for the protection of human health and the environment by providing technical assistance to support recovery planning of public health and infrastructure, such as wastewater treatment plants. The agency supplies technical assistance for long-term cleanups in a bid to minimise public health threats, environmental surveillance, site assessments, decontamination, and disposal of waste hazards such as radioactive waste and chemical spills. The agency has approximately 15,000 employees and an annual budget of around $9.1 billion.

Zeldin is a key and willing component in Trump's climate agenda which includes boosting fossil fuel expansion and rolling back environmental regulation for the oil and gas industry. A zealous Trump ally, Zeldin prominently defended Trump during his first impeachment hearings and in the seven impeachment deposition transcripts released, as of November 2019, Zeldin was referenced more than 550 times, a prolific contributor. He was also one of 126 Republican members of the House of Representatives to sign an amicus brief presented to United States Supreme Court contesting the results of the 2020 election, in which Biden defeated Trump.

(*amicus brief; a legal document filed by a person or organisation not directly involved in a case, who wishes to provide the court with additional information or arguments).

In 2022, he supported an amendment to cut the EPA's budget, voted for pulling the U.S. out of the UN Framework Convention on Climate Change, and voted against investment in conservation and restoration of wildlife.

Within the first three months of his tenure at the EPA, Zeldin had sought to re-frame the purpose of the agency and push for substantial deregulation and energy production in lieu of public health and environmental protections. He announced plans to repeal a substantial amount of crucial environmental regulations, including protections for wetlands, and pollution limits on emissions. Zeldin has also announced that the agency plans to cut jobs, eliminate its scientific research arm, and reduce the EPA's budget by 65%.

During his Senate confirmation hearing Zeldin stated that climate change is a real issue and needs to be addressed. In early 2025 in an interview with *CBS News'* Face the Nation, Zeldin said he *"can absolutely guarantee Trump administration deregulations won't have adverse health impacts on people and the environment."*

In March 2025, The Environmental Protection Agency said it would "formally reconsider" a landmark 2009 endangerment finding by the agency that greenhouse gases are a danger to public health.

By April 15, 2025, nearly 70 coal power plants were exempted from regulations on mercury pollution merely by sending an email request to the agency. Zeldin has said these exemptions will also be available for coal-burning power plant's coal ash pollution.

In response to Trump's executive order on "ending radical and wasteful government DEI programs and preferences," the EPA is looking to eliminate all positions at the agency focused on diversity, equity and inclusion and environmental justice.

Administrator of the Small Business Administration

Kelly Lyn Loeffler – November 27, 1970

Estimated net worth 2024 - $1 Billion

In March 2020, Loeffler and other senators attended a classified briefing that set out the possible severity and impacts on goods and services from the COVID-19 pandemic. Shortly after, she and her husband sold around $20 million in stocks in companies that would be hit hardest by the pandemic and purchased in areas that could benefit such as teleworking software.

Insisting there was nothing wrong with her transactions, Loeffler said a third-party adviser had made the decisions on her behalf without her knowledge and vowed to liquidate all her individual stock holdings in a bid to put an end to the accusations. The Department of Justice ultimately closed an insider trading inquiry into Loeffler.

Early Years

Loeffler and her brother were born in Bloomington, Illinois, to Don and Lynda (née Munsell) Loeffler. They were raised on their family's large third generation corn and soybean farm in Stanford, Illinois. After graduating from, Olympia High School in Stanford in 1988 she went on to be first in her family to graduate college. Loeffler obtained her Bachelor of Science in marketing from the University of Illinois at Urbana-Champaign's Gies College of Business in 1992.

She then worked for Toyota for several years as a district account manager and in 1999, successfully completed her Master of Business Administration (MBA) in international finance and marketing from the DePaul Kellstadt Gradutae School of Business. Loeffler had inherited some farmland from her grandparents and was able to use the land as collateral for a mortgage to pay for her MBA course.

After earning her MBA, Loeffler worked for a number of different companies including Citibank, William Blair & Company, and the Crossroads Group. In 2002 she secured a position in investor relations with the Intercontinental Exchange (ICE), a commodity and financial service provider which serves as the parent to the New York Stock Exchange. Loeffler was promoted to senior vice president of investor relations and corporate communications and in 2018 became the co-founder and CEO of subsidiary company Bakkt.

Loeffler married husband Jeff Sprecher, who is CEO of Intercontinental Exchange, in 2004. In 2013 they purchased a 15,000 square-foot (1,400 m^2) estate in Tuxedo Park, Atlanta. This estate was, at that time, the most expensive residential real estate transaction ever recorded in Atlanta. They have four additional homes and a condominium.

Political Ascension

When Georgian Republican Senator Johnny Isakson retired at the end of 2019, Governor Brian Kemp appointed Loeffler to fill Isakson's Senate seat until the next regularly scheduled statewide elections. She then left her position as CEO of Bakkt and, after being sworn in to the Senate, took office in January 2020.

Loeffler ran for office in the 2020 Georgia U.S. Senate special elections in a bid to hold her seat for a further two years. Republican Senator David Perdue, who was also running for office, lost his seat in the special election and as Loeffler had gained second position she was propelled to the rank of senior Senator; a position she held for just under three weeks until the runoff election.

As none of the candidates running had received over 50% of the vote in the special election the first and second placed candidates, Democrat Reverend Raphael Warnock and Republican Loeffler, participated in a runoff election. Loeffler was ultimately defeated on January 5, 2021, by Warnock, who gained 51% of the vote.

Following her loss in the 2020 Georgia U.S. Senate special election, Loeffler founded 'Greater Georgia', a company that advocated for increased voter participation, conservative political marketing, and changes to voting laws legislation. Loeffler joined the board of directors of Public Square, an online presence marketed towards conservatives, before becoming co-chair of Trump's 2024 inaugural committee, alongside property developer Steven Witkoff, who now holds the position of special Middle East Envoy.

On December 5, 2024, Trump announced Loeffler as his nominee for Administrator of the Small Business Administration. On February 19, 2025, the Senate confirmed her nomination in a 52–46 vote.

The Most Conservative Republican

Loeffler, as the head of the U.S. Small Business Administration (SBA), is responsible for overseeing and managing the agency's operations, which support small businesses and entrepreneurs. She will also be responsible for managing the SBA's many programs, including loan guarantees, counselling, and other various assistance services. The agency had approximately 6,500 employees and an annual budget of $8.3 billion, prior to the recently announced 43% cuts.

Loeffler is a wealthy businesswoman and generous political donor with extremely limited political experience. She does however have many successful years in business as a senior vice president of investor relations and corporate communications, a former CEO for Bakkt, and once co-owned the WNBA team, the 'Atlanta Dream'.

In her brief year in the Senate Loeffler referred to herself as 'the most conservative Republican' in the Senate and quickly aligned herself with Trump. She voted in line with Trump's ideological position 80% of the time including the repeal of the Affordable Care Act, opposition to abortion, she supported an adoption agency that opposed LGBTQ+ parents, opposed an assault weapons ban, and supported the Mexico-United States border wall.

During the 2024 U.S. presidential election, Loeffler was a top donor to Trump, having contributed more than $4.9 million to his re-election effort.

In 2010, Loeffler purchased a minority stake in the Atlanta Dream basketball team, a member of the Women's National Basketball Association. In 2011 she and Mary Brock, wife of former Coca-Cola Enterprises CEO John Brock, bought the team outright. Loeffler attacked the teams support of the "Black Lives Matter movement" calling for team members to not bring their politics into the game. An *Atlanta Journal-Constitution* article reported on Loeffler's objections to the league honoring the Black Lives Matter movement on the court and on players' warm-up uniforms. This did not sit well with the team.

During her 2020 Senate campaign the controversy with the Atlanta Dream players came back to haunt her. Team members openly campaigned for Loeffler's Democratic opponent in her ultimately unsuccessful 2020 Georgia senate race.

In February 2021 Loeffler sold her stake in the team; the sale had been anticipated for some time. Players, on the Dream roster and within the league, had publicly criticised Loeffler for her attacks on the Black Lives Matter movement.

U.S. Trade Representative

Jamieson Greer – March 4, 1979

Estimated net worth - $3 Million

During Greer's confirmation enquiries some Republican Senators were anxious about the proposed White House Tariffs and the imposition of "extreme tariffs" that could backfire on the U.S.

Although many fear Greer will take an aggressive approach to tariffs, some were hopeful for a steadier and more co-operative strategy that included opening access to new markets through new trade deals. Senators pointed to the fact that Greer is an eloquent, well-respected French-speaking global trade expert.

Early Years

Greer, a Mormon, was born in Paradise, California and is one of five children of Michael and Shannon Greer. He attended Paradise High graduating in 1998 and then for the next two years served a mission for The Church of Jesus Christ of Latter-day Saints in Brussels. On the completion of his missionary work he enrolled in Brigham Young University where he completed a Bachelor of Arts degree in International Studies. He also holds a Juris Doctor from the University of Virginia School of Law as well as a joint master's degree in Global Business Law from l'Institut d'Etudes Politiques de Paris and l'Université de Paris I Panthéon-Sorbonne.

Greer served in the U.S. Air Force Judge Advocate General's Corps from 2008 to 2012. During a deployment to Iraq, he held the position of chief of military justice and was posted in Incirlik Air Base in Türkiye where he served as the area defense counsel representing U.S. military personnel in criminal courts, administrative hearings, and adverse personnel actions at U.S. military installations abroad. Additionally, he served a two-year term on the Air Force Law Review editorial board.

After leaving the Air Force, Greer joined International Trade practice group, Skadden, Arps, Slate, Meagher & Flom LLP and Affiliates, as an associate. Through Federal agencies and courts, he represented corporate clients to secure trade remedies such as antidumping and countervailing duties. Moving onto international trade and national security practice group, Kirkland & Ellis, Greer advised clients concerning compliance issues with export control, sanctions, and customs regulations. Joining King & Spalding in 2020 as a partner in the International trade team, Greer focused on assisting companies use international trade laws and policies to achieve geopolitically sustainable business models.

He has extensive experience representing clients in the area of international trade litigation before the Department of Commerce, the International Trade Commission, and federal courts. He has also advocated for clients before U.S. Congress, senior officials, and government agencies with jurisdiction over international trade matters.

Jamieson and his wife Marlo have five children together and live in the Washington, D.C. area.

Political Ascension

Greer served in the U.S. Trade department (USTR) during Trump's first term as Chief of Staff to USTR Ambassador Robert Lighthizer. He was directly involved in the first Trump Administration's implementation of tariffs on China and the subsequent negotiation of the U.S.-China "Phase One Agreement." * He also played a significant role in USTR's efforts in negotiating and obtaining Congressional approval for the U.S.-Mexico-Canada Trade Agreement.

*(*Phase One Agreement was an enforceable agreement on trade deals between the U.S. and China requiring structural reforms and other changes to China's economic and trade regime).*

Leading diplomatic talks in 2018 Greer renegotiated the U.S.-South Korea free trade deal and ensured congressional support for the U.S.-Japan Trade Agreement in 2019.

Between Trump's first and second terms, Greer joined Legal firm King & Spalding as a partner in the International Trade team. He specialised in dealing with unfair trade practices, navigation of the U.S.- China strategic competition, compliance with national security policies, regulatory aspects of cross-border transactions, and influencing U.S. government trade policy.

On February 26, 2025, the U.S. Senate voted to confirm Jamieson Greer as United States Trade Representative in a vote of 56-43.

Co-operative diplomat

The Office of the United States Trade Representative has principal responsibility for development and coordination of U.S. international trade, commodity and direct investment policy. The agency is also the main trade negotiator for the U.S. in bilateral, regional and multilateral trade and investment agreements.

Jamieson played a key role during Trump's First Term as chief of staff to U.S. Trade Representative Robert Lighthizer gaining valuable experience and respect from his peers. His extensive legal background in international trade, regulation and negotiation all add to his impressive skillset making him an obvious choice for the role.

The trade representative's office is required, by law, to report directly to the president, however Trump announced that Commerce secretary, Howard Lutnick, would oversee tariff and trade policy and that the U.S. trade representative would report directly to Lutnick.

Trump has also appointed Peter Navarro, Trump's former director of the White House National Trade Council, to be his senior counsellor for trade and manufacturing in the White House.

Republican Senator Ron Wyden has suggested that Greer would be struggling to have a say when it came to trade policy, considering the amount of people Trump has given power to on the issue: *"There are an awful lot of trade cooks in that kitchen,"* Wyden said.

At his Senate confirmation hearing, Greer emphasised that he would report directly to the president.

MISC. NON-CABINET ROLES

White House Press Secretary

Karoline Claire Leavitt – August 24, 1997

Estimated Net Worth 2025 - $6 Million

Leavitt and her boss, White House communications director Steven Cheung, are said to have a "good guy, bad guy" dynamic whereby Leavitt is the diplomatic responder to press enquiries and Cheung "knocks heads together."

When she receives enquiries that refer to opinions of ethical experts, she requests the enquirers source, Googles the information, copy and pastes any information from Wikipedia and hands that information along to Cheung.

Cheung then emails the enquirer back with the Google search results and a retort of, *"These experts, a--hole?"* Leavitt has said it's the favourite part of her job.

Early Years

Leavitt was born in Atkinson, New Hampshire, the youngest of three children to Bob and Erin Leavitt. Her family owns an ice cream stand in Atkinson and a used truck dealership in Plaistow. Leavitt attended Central Catholic, High School, a private Catholic School in Lawrence, Massachusetts. She received a softball scholarship to attend Saint Anslem College university where in 2015 she began her university studies majoring in communications and minoring in political science.

She had a short internship with *NBC Sports Boston*, later shifting her focus toward political journalism after she became involved with the New Hampshire Institute of Politics in her second year at university. As an institute ambassador, she was assigned to *Fox News* on campus during the 2016 presidential primary, interned in the White House correspondence office and *ABC* affiliate *WMUR-TV* as a news assistant.

Political Ascension

Shortly after graduating from university in 2019 Leavitt was offered a job as one of three assistant press secretaries to Trump's fourth Press Secretary Kayleigh McEnany and ascended to the rank of assistant White House Press Secretary.

After Trump's 2020 election loss, Leavitt moved to Capitol Hill and took a job as communications director for New York Republican Senator Elise Stefanik. She watched her new boss consolidate the Republican party behind Trump and his 2020 election loss denial campaign. Leavitt quickly learned from Stefanik that voters in the MAGA movement will support you when you take a tough stand to fight for the cause.

She returned to New Hampshire with a dream of becoming a congresswoman and set out to campaign in the 2022 midterms for a position in New Hampshire's first congressional district. Leavitt's campaign was based largely on her limited experience within the Trump administration, and her support of Trump's election fraud assertions. She sought to be viewed as the most pro-Trump candidate in the Republican primary.

Leavitt won her primary vote but eventually lost the election to the Democratic incumbent. Following this loss, she joined Trump's super PAC, MAGA Inc. and starting doing TV campaigns. She also featured in a video for Project 2025 aimed at training political appointees on how to counter the federal bureaucracy.

Leavitt met her future husband, Nicholas Riccio a real estate developer 32 years her senior, through a mutual friend at a restaurant during her 2022 congressional campaign. They were engaged in December 2023. By mid-2024, she had been appointed as national press secretary for Trump's 2024 presidential campaign. However, she was also pregnant and was expecting a baby in July 2024. She gave birth to her son on July 10 and was offered a month's parental leave; she refused requesting only 10 days as "she was in a hurry." Three days after Leavitt gave birth, a would-be assassin opened fire at Trump's rally in Butler, Pennsylvania. Leavitt went back to work that day.

On November 15, 2024, president-elect Trump named Leavitt as his White House Press Secretary; Senate confirmation is not required for this position. She is the youngest White House press secretary in history.

She married Nicholas Riccio in January 2025.

First White House Press Secretary?

The Office of the Press Secretary is responsible for gathering and disseminating information to the president, the White House staff and the media. Leavitt as press secretary is the chief spokesperson for the president and his administration and advises the president on press strategy and press relations, briefs the press daily, and coordinates with press offices in other agencies.

Leavitt has prior experience in the role as assistant press secretary, communications director and was national press secretary for Trump's successful 2024 presidential campaign. She is a true believer, willing to repeat anything she's told by the administration, and repeats Trump's "alternate facts" ad nauseum. She supports increasing inhibitive requirements on voting, Trump's immigration policies and vehemently opposed vaccine mandates. Leavitt has falsely stated that Trump is the legitimate winner of the 2020 presidential election and that "irregularities and chaos" occurred as a result of deceptive precautions to do with the COVID-19 pandemic. Leavitt ticks all the boxes for Trump's first press secretary of his second term.

Trump had multiple press secretaries during his first four-year term, including Sean Spicer, Sarah Huckabee Sanders, Stephanie Grisham and Kayleigh McEnany.

Leavitt gave her first press conference on January 28, 2025, where she falsely stated that $50 million in taxpayer dollars had been intended for use in funding condoms in the Gaza Strip.

They were in fact sent to Gaza Province in Mozambique to protect people against HIV.

Trump reaffirmed this false statement the next day during a media conference.

Border Czar

White House Executive Associate Director of Enforcement and Removal Operations

Thomas Douglas Homan – November 28, 1961

Estimated net worth – $10 Million

Homan has described himself as "a lifelong Catholic" and has been described as "a devout mass-goer" nonetheless he was critical of Pope Francis' (1936-2025) position on immigration.

In a 2025 letter to U.S. bishops, Pope Francis wrote, *"The rightly formed conscience cannot fail to make a critical judgment and express its disagreement with any measure that tacitly or explicitly identifies the illegal status of some migrants with criminality."* Homan responded with, *"I wish he'd stick to the Catholic Church and fix that and leave border enforcement to us,"* offering *"He's got a wall around the Vatican, does he not?"* Homan added.

Early Years

Homan was born in West Carthage, New York into a Roman Catholic family of seven children to Frederick Leroy Homan and Doris I. (née Gibeau) Homan. Each of Homan's brothers and sisters became either a police officer, firefighter or a nurse. After receiving an associate degree in criminal justice from Jefferson, Community College Homan went on to complete a bachelor's degree in criminal justice from the SUNY Polytechnic Institute.

In 1983, Homan like his father and grandfather before him, became a West Carthage police officer and in 1984, Homan joined the then 'Immigration and Naturalization Service' (INS) serving as a Border Patrol agent, investigator, and supervisor. In 1988, he became a Special Agent posted in Phoenix, Arizona, and climbed through the ranks of Supervisory Special Agent and Deputy Assistant Director for Investigations.

By 1999, Homan had taken on the role of Assistant District Director for Investigations (ADDI) in San Antonio, Texas, and after three years transferred to the ADDI position in Dallas, Texas. In 2003 Immigration and Customs Enforcement (ICE) became one of the new agencies formed after most of the functions of INS were transferred to three newly formed agencies under the banner of the Department of Homeland Security. Homan was named as the ICE Assistant Special Agent in Charge in Dallas, Texas, and later as the Deputy Special Agent in Charge.

In March of 2009, Homan accepted the position of assistant director for Enforcement at ICE Headquarters in Washington D.C. and was subsequently promoted to deputy executive associate director of Enforcement and Removal Operations (ERO).

Homan and his wife Elizabeth met when they were in High School and married in 1980. They have four children together.

Political Ascension

Homan was appointed by President Barack Obama as Immigration and Customs Enforcement's executive associate director of ERO in 2013. Homan began asserting in 2014 that separating children from their caregivers would be an effective way of discouraging illegal border crossings. He maintained that parents don't want to be separated from their children, and this made separation an effective tool for immigration enforcement. The Obama administration did not pursue Homan's ideas for separating children from their parents as a deterrent to illegal immigration. In 2015, former President Obama awarded him a Presidential Rank Award as a Distinguished Executive, the highest civil service award in the nation.

On January 30, 2017, Trump appointed Homan as acting ICE director for his first presidential term team. By May 2017, Homan announced that ICE had arrested over 41,000 people by the end of April, an increase of some 38% compared to the same period in the prior year. On November 14, 2017, Trump nominated Homan for ICE director.

Homan's 2014 ideas for separating children from their parents as a deterrent was appealing to the Trump administration and in April 2018 Trump's "zero tolerance" policy on immigration, including the prosecution of parents and the separation of children from their families was announced. Homan participated in a May 2018 press conference announcing that the policy was going into effect. The policy was highly controversial and very unpopular, leading to dozens of demonstrations and the Office of the United Nations High Commissioner for Human Rights calling for an immediate halt to the policy.

After just 16 months serving as the most controversial acting ICE director in the agency's brief history, Homan retired from his position in June 2018. Homan went on to testify before the U.S. House Oversight Committee in 2019 regarding the Trump administration family separation policy.

Homan accepted the position of News commentator with *Fox News* and in February 2022 joined the Heritage Foundation as a contributor to its Project 2025. Homan is said to have contributed to the section on immigration which proposes mass arrests, detentions and deportations of undocumented immigrants across the nation, though his name is not specifically listed on any particular area of the narrative.

On November 10, 2024, president-elect Trump announced that Homan would be joining his incoming administration as the "border czar."

Good at a Bad Job

Immigration enforcement is the largest single area of responsibility for Enforcement and Removal Operations (ERO). Though the agency has significant assets near the border, the majority of its immigration enforcement mission takes place in the interior of the country. ERO coordinates closely with law enforcement partners and one of the most notable coordination and partnership efforts within ERO involves the biometric and biographic identification of priority undocumented aliens who are in federal, state, and local prisons and jails. ERO has administrative authority to arrest individuals deemed a threat to public safety on their unlawful immigration status even without additional criminal charges. ICE has approximately 21,000 employees and an estimated budget for the year 2025 of $10 billion.

Homan has nearly four decades experience in law enforcement and immigration deportation. He held the position of acting ICE director under the first Trump administration and appears to hold the same views on immigration as Trump. He is willing to do what needs to be done to enact Trump's agenda. And as the *Washington Post* reported in 2015, "Thomas Homan deports people. And he's really good at it."

On May 14, 2003, police found an abandoned trailer in Victoria, Texas, where over 70 migrants had been smuggled in a sealed truck. Seventeen died from suffocation inside, and two more died later. Homan had been set to deliver a speech in Dallas that morning but changed plans when informed about the trailer instead flying to Victoria. A Texas Ranger guided him through the crime scene and into the trailer where the victims were found. One of the deceased was a man whose 5-year-old child had died in his arms.

He still includes the story in his speeches, partly to challenge the belief that immigration enforcement officials, like himself, are indifferent. "This is something I'll never forget," Homan said. "At the time, I had a 5-year-old son."

In March 2025, two planes carrying individuals alleged by the Trump administration to be Venezuelan gang members, were deported to El Salvador, defying a court order that had blocked the expulsions. Homan told the media that the deportations proceeded because the court order was issued after the planes had already crossed into international waters. Homan further declared, *"Another flight every day. [...] We are not stopping. I don't care what the judges think."*

National Security Adviser

Michael George Glen Waltz – January 31, 1974

Estimated net worth – $2.5 to 10.5 Million

In early May 2025 Trump removed Mike Waltz from his post as national security adviser and is slated to be nominated by Trump as ambassador to the United Nations. Secretary of State Marco Rubio is now the acting National Security Adviser until he is appointed permanently, or until Trump nominates another candidate for the position.

Early Years

Waltz was born in Boynton Beach, Florida, and was raised solely by his mother in Jacksonville, Florida. His family had a strong navy background as his father and grandfather were both Navy Chiefs. He graduated from Stanton High School, Jacksonville, in 1992 and earned a Bachelor of Arts degree in international studies from the Virginia Military Institute in 1996, graduating with honors as a Distinguished Military Graduate.

Waltz joined the U.S. Army in 1996 and after successfully graduating from Ranger School he went on to graduate from the Special Forces Qualification Course in 2000. He served two years as an active-duty Special Forces officer with multiple tours in the Middle East, Afghanistan, and Africa. Waltz received four Bronze Stars, including two for valor for his actions in combat.

Waltz alternated between combat deployments and work as a defense policy director in the Pentagon for the former president George W Bush's administrations for secretaries of defense Donald Rumsfeld and Robert Gates and as a counterterrorism advisor to Vice President Dick Cheney in the White House.

In 2010, Waltz co-founded the intelligence analytics and training company, Metis Solutions. The company quickly grew to 400 employees and won several coveted government contracts to train special forces in Afghanistan, including a program to develop artisanal mining operations in militarily strategic villages. The company was eventually bought out in November 2020 by Pacific Architects and Engineers (PAE) for $92 million. Shortly before its acquisition by PAE, Metis Solutions was awarded a $26 million contract from the U.S. military on countering threats from terrorist financing and money laundering.

Walz spent some time as a security commentator for the *Fox News* Channel where he became a recognised voice on global threats and defense issues. And in 2014, he published a book, *Warrior Diplomat: A Green Beret's Battles from Washington to Afghanistan* that was inspired by his military and political experiences. All proceeds from the book go to veteran support organisations, including the Green Beret Foundation. In 2022 he co-authored *Dawn of the Brave*, a children's book that emphasised the values of service and patriotism.

Waltz married Dr. Julia Nesheiwat in August 2021, a combat veteran who has served in multiple presidential administrations, including as Trump's Homeland Security Advisor 2020-2021. They have a young son together and Walz has a daughter from a previous relationship. The family resides in St. Johns County, Florida.

Political Ascension

Waltz ran for Florida's 6th congressional district in 2018 after incumbent Republican Ron DeSantis, retired after being elected governor of Florida. He won the Republican primary before facing Democratic nominee Nancy Soderberg in the general election. Waltz won with 56.31% of the vote to Soderberg's 43.69% making him the first Green Beret to be elected to Congress. Waltz went on to serve in the succeeding three Congresses. During his second term in Congress Waltz retired from the Army at the rank of Colonel.

On January 20, 2025, Waltz resigned from the U.S. House of Representatives in order to take up his appointment with the Trump administration. He assumed office on the same day.

Taken Down by Group Chat

The national security advisor role is not a cabinet-level position and therefore does not require Senate confirmation. It is a staff position in the Executive office of the President.

The role of national security adviser is changeable depending on current affairs during the President's term. The main roles are to help guide the President's decision-making on matters of homeland security, national defense, and foreign affairs. As national security advisor Walz was a member of the National Security Council (NSC) that works out of the White House and is formally led by the president or, when the president is away, the vice president.

Shortly after becoming National Security Advisor, Waltz reversed his previous strong stance of supporting a ban on TikTok in the U.S. even though he had previously branded TikTok "Chinese spyware." This reversal ensured alignment with Trump's position.

In December 2020, Waltz was one of 126 Republican members of the House of Representatives to sign the amicus brief that supported a lawsuit that contested the results of the 2020 presidential election, in which Donald Trump was defeated. Waltz did ultimately vote to confirm the electoral victory of Joe Biden however he did vote against the formation of a January 6 commission to investigate the Capitol riots.

Waltz's vast military, security and intelligence experience both in the private and governmental sectors makes him a valid choice for the NSA role. He also has extensive Congressional experience holding a Senate seat for four terms. He has also proven to be willingly changeable to show his loyalty to Trump.

Nevertheless, none of these attributes were enough to shield him from the fallout of the "signal-gate"' scandal.

Waltz was removed from his role and Secretary of State Marco Rubio was appointed acting National Security Adviser on May 1, 2025.

Waltz was removed from his post as national security adviser after criticism from the "signal-gate" scandal escalated. Waltz mistakenly added editor-in-chief Jeffrey Goldberg from the *Atlantic magazine* to a group chat where sensitive military plans were being discussed. The incident sparked national security concerns as Pentagon regulations specifically prohibit the use of Signal and similar messaging apps for sharing classified information. A prohibition one would think wouldn't need to be pointed out to security professionals.

Trump's decision to oust Waltz and no other senior level contributors to the Signal chat, is argued by some to be the product of a slow accumulation of frustration with Waltz. Waltz has been accused of participating in a meeting with Israeli Prime Minister Benjamin Netanyahu about possible military strikes against Iran prior to an Oval Office meeting between the Israeli leader and Trump. Trump is said to have not been consulted about these discussions. Walz and Trump's positions on several fronts are believed to not align and it could be argued that Trump took the opportunity, that the "signal gate" scandal gave him, to get rid of Waltz without having to fire him.

This political embarrassment will no doubt be a feature of his Senate confirmation hearing for the UN post.

Director of the Federal Bureau of Intelligence

Kashyap Pramod Vinod Patel – February 25, 1980

Estimated net worth 2024 - $5.9 Million

During Patel's initial tenure with the Department of Justice in 2012, he briefly served as a representative of the Criminal Division in proceedings related to the 2012 Benghazi attack*. He was allegedly removed from the case due to disagreements with the Columbia U.S. Attorney's Office. Subsequently, Patel claimed to have been asked to serve as the lead prosecutor in the matter. In his book, *Government Gangsters: The Deep State, the Truth, and the Battle for Our Democracy*, Patel asserts that he had been invited to join the trial team prosecuting Ahmed Abu Khattala, a militia leader involved in the Libyan civil conflict; however, *The New York Times* reported that no such offer had been made to him.

(*Benghazi attack was a 2012 terrorist attack on the U.S. Special Mission in Benghazi, Libya)

Early Years

Patel is of Ugandan Indian descent. His family were among those who faced ethnic persecution and were expelled by Ugandan dictator Idi Amin in 1972. The family first immigrated to Canada before finally settling permanently in the U.S. Patel was born in Garden City, New York. He attended Garden City High School and in 2002 graduated from the University of Richmond with a degree in criminal justice and history. He earned a certificate in international law from the University College London and completed his Juris Doctor degree at the Pace University School of Law in 2005. In 2003 Patel participated in the American Bar's diversity initiative, "Judicial Intern Opportunity Program," when he was a student at Pace University.

Patel's professional career began in Miami-Dade, Florida where he worked as a public defender from 2006 to 2014. He served as a trial attorney at the U.S. Department of Justice from 2014 to 2017, where he gained experience in national security matters.

He left the Department of Justice in early 2017 and would later say the reason for his departure had been the department's response to the 2016 presidential election.

Patel has never married.

Political Ascension

In April 2017 under Trump's first presidential term, Patel was assigned to the House Permanent Select Committee on Intelligence, then led by Representative Devin Nunes. He was senior counsel to Nunes for two years, assisting with the committee's widely criticised inquiry into the FBI's Russia investigation into interference in the 2016 U.S. presidential elections. Patel was the primary author of a 2018 memo that emerged from that investigation, alleging that FBI officials abused their authority into an investigation into links between associates of Trump and Russian officials.

The memo, relying mostly on unverified claims made by a British intelligence officer, was widely seen as an effort to undermine Special Counsel Robert Mueller's investigation into Trump's involvement in the Russian election tampering scandal. While the memo's reliability was highly questioned, it bolstered Patel's standing among Trump allies.

In 2019, Patel served as Trump's senior director for counterterrorism on the National Security Council (NSC) where he reportedly clashed with officials who weren't always as willing as Patel to side with what they thought were the then-president's more extreme views. His colleagues on the council considered him inexperienced for the position and a "must-hire, directed by the president." Nevertheless, in February 2020, Patel was appointed senior adviser for Trump's directors of national intelligence.

During Trump's final months in office in November 2020, Patel was promoted to chief of staff to acting Defense Secretary Christopher Miller.

Following Trump's defeat in the 2020 election, Patel established the Kash Network, a nonprofit organisation that supports legal and educational initiatives for individuals aligned with Trump, including whistleblowers and Americans claiming defamation. He also sold merchandise branded with "K$H," which expressed support for Trump and individuals involved in the January 6 Capitol riot.

In 2021, Patel formed Trishul LLC, a national security, defense, and intelligence consulting firm. According to Patel's financial disclosure, filed to the Office of Government Ethics prior to his 2025 confirmation hearing, Trishul earned more than $2.1 million in consulting fees in 2024. Trishul consulting clients included the Trump's Media and Technology Group, the Embassy of Qatar and Russell Vought 's Center for Renewing America.

After the FBI search and seizure of classified documents at Trump's residence Mar-a-Lago, Patel claimed that Trump had declassified the seized documents. As part of the FBI Investigation of Trump's handling of government documents, that led to Trump being indicted for allegedly withholding White House documents, Patel appeared twice before a grand jury in October 2022, repeatedly pleading the Fifth Amendment. Prosecutors offered Patel immunity in November, securing his testimony.

On November 30, 2024, Trump named Patel as his nominee as Director of the FBI, by January 2025, nearly two dozen Republican government officials had sent a letter to senators urging them to reject Patel's nomination.

On February 20, Patel was confirmed by the Senate in a 51 to 49 vote. All Republican senators voted in favour of his confirmation except Susan Collins, who expressed concern over his past criticism of the FBI and the potential for retaliation against agents involved in the January 6 investigations, and Lisa Murkowski, who opposed him for not resisting the Trump administration's request for a list of those agents. Every Democratic senator voted against his nomination.

Only days later Patel was also made acting director of the Bureau of Alcohol, Tobacco, Firearms, and Explosives.

A Different Kind of Director

The FBI is a law enforcement and national security agency that gathers, uses, and shares intelligence with the goal of protecting the American public and upholding the Constitution. Its core responsibilities are enforcing federal laws and safeguarding national security. Patel, as FBI director, oversees the agency's daily operations and overall leadership and answers directly to the U.S. Attorney General.

Patel has had an interesting career ascension and since 2012 has weathered several controversies. Early in his career as a prosecutor for the Department of Justice he was removed from a case and misrepresented the facts about being asked to be lead prosecutor. While serving as Senior Counsel for the House Permanent Select Committee on Intelligence, he was involved in an investigation related to a contentious memo he authored. The memo made unverified allegations against FBI officials, accusing them of misconduct during their investigation into connections between Trump associates and Russian officials. He was regarded as inexperienced and a "must-hire by his colleagues while in the role of Deputy Assistant to the President and Senior Director for Counterterrorism at the National Security Council.

However, after being granted limited immunity by the Justice Department in the Mar-a-Lago "classified" documents scandal, he continued to insist that Trump had declassified the documents, arguing that no laws had been broken.

Patel lacks senior law enforcement experience and has been involved in a series of controversies throughout his career. Nonetheless, few individuals have demonstrated the same degree of loyalty to Trump as Patel has.

For decades, prior FBI directors participated in a daily 8:30 a.m. "director's brief," where top intelligence and law enforcement updates gathered from agents and analysts nationwide were presented. Additionally, every Wednesday afternoon, a secure video conference was held with field office leaders across the country to discuss key bureau priorities and share information.

It has been reported that Patel now receives the "director's brief" only twice a week and no longer conducts the weekly Wednesday afternoon video teleconference with FBI leadership.

On October 15, 1976, in reaction to the astonishing 48-year term of J. Edgar Hoover, Congress passed Public Law 94-503, that limits an FBI Director to a single term of no longer than 10 years. Ten years is still a long time.

In the 2020 Nigeria hostage rescue operation, Patel played a controversial role by incorrectly telling the Department of Defense that Secretary of State Mike Pompeo had secured approval to enter Nigerian airspace. As the aircraft neared landing, Secretary of Defense Mark Esper discovered that no such authorisation had been obtained. Although the SEAL Team was eventually granted permission to land, the miscommunication put hostage Philip Walton and several Navy SEALs at serious risk.

In early April 2025, Patel was removed as acting director of the Bureau of Alcohol, Tobacco, Firearms and Explosives due to concerns that it was overly burdensome. He was succeeded by Daniel P. Driscoll, the Secretary of the Army. The decision to place the FBI director in charge of the ATF had been unconventional, as the agency has historically operated under its own independent leadership.

Tangled Webs

By definition, President Donald Trump regards all those around him as minions, positioning himself as the ultimate master. He acknowledges no equals, not even those with the resources or influence to manipulate his agenda or secure a place within his inner circle. However, effective governance within a constitutional framework requires the president to build alliances in both the House and the Senate.

Not all of Trump's appointments were unjustified; some individuals bring substantial experience relevant to their roles, even if not gained within government agencies. Nevertheless, Trump also appointed figures who lacked the experience or competence to hold key positions, whose primary qualifications seemed to be loyalty, political support, or mere association and who have extraordinarily little comprehension of the everyday struggles of the average American. The repercussions of their actions are now being felt not only in the United States, but across the globe.

Fox News has been widely recognised for its dedicated support of Donald Trump, providing him with extensive coverage throughout both his first and second terms. As of now, at least 23 former *Fox News* employees have taken positions within the White House and federal government, including Secretary of Defense Pete Hegseth, former National Security Adviser and current U.N. ambassador nominee Mike Walz, and Secretary of

Transportation Sean Duffy. This pattern reflects Trump's apparent preference for certain individuals, who may lack traditional political experience but demonstrate loyalty, a confrontational style, and strong media presence.

Trump's second administration has been described as one of the wealthiest governing groups in American history. This has raised concerns about potential conflicts of interest, particularly in light of Trump's pledge to represent the "forgotten men and women" of the country, many of whom live on median annual incomes ranging from approximately $30,000 to $88,000. Critics question whether a Cabinet and White House staff composed largely of extremely wealthy individuals can genuinely relate to the economic challenges faced by everyday Americans. Yet the issue extends beyond wealth or inexperience; it's about how power is maintained, loyalty is rewarded, and institutions are reshaped around the needs of a single figure. This leads us to a deeper pattern at play: one best explained by the "Red Queen Theory."

(Named in reference to the Red Queen in 'Lewis Carroll's fantasy 1871 novel Through the Looking-Glass)

The Red Queen Theory suggests that in a constantly changing environment, players must evolve, adapt, and compete to survive especially as their political adversaries are doing the same. In political systems, this dynamic often produces strategies rooted not in policy or governance, but in survival, misinformation, calculated chaos, and shifting alliances. The pressure to stay ahead of the opposition forces leaders to continuously reinvent themselves and their teams, often at the expense of stability or competence.

Enter the non-gender specific Political Red Queen (PRQ), a survivalist who crafts policy, enacts laws, and makes promises not necessarily to govern effectively, but to fortify their political standing. The PRQ disrupts the usual processes of political accountability by building parasitic and symbiotic relationships, relying on loyal subordinates to execute decisions and defend their image. Their influence depends heavily on coordinating resources they don't directly control and leveraging allies outside traditional structures, all while avoiding blame through ambiguity and plausible deniability.

A historical example of this type of governance can be seen in the German Nazi regime, where bureaucratic chaos was a feature, not a flaw. Orders from leadership were often intentionally vague, encouraging competition among subordinates and fostering an environment where initiative, no matter how extreme, was rewarded. Responsibilities overlapped, leading to internal rivalries and duplication of efforts. It was a system designed to maintain power through disorder, while always allowing the leadership to claim distance from unpopular outcomes.

While vastly different in historical and moral terms, Trump's administration displays structural similarities in the way it rewards loyalty, blurs authority, and tolerates, even encourages, factional conflict. In both his first and second terms, Trump increasingly surrounded himself with individuals whose primary qualifications were allegiance, visibility, and media savvy.

Figures like Pete Hegseth, a television commentator with no prior governmental leadership experience but deep loyalty and on-screen presence, was elevated to a key defense role. Kash Patel, known more for his loyalty and willingness to challenge intelligence narratives than for deep policy expertise, has emerged as a powerful operative in national security matters. Linda McMahon, a former wrestling executive, was appointed to lead the Department of Education, bringing branding clout and personal loyalty rather than public-sector experience.

The trend continued with rising political allies like Kristi Noem, whose ideological alignment and public support of Trump propelled her to the head of homeland security. Perhaps most strikingly, Robert F. Kennedy Jr., a long-time Democrat and staunch conspiracy theorist, is now leading the department of health and human services demonstrating the extent to which loyalty to Trump's current political posture, not background or consistency, defined their suitability for high office.

These appointments reflect the PRQ's modus operandi: surround yourself not with specialists, but with loyalists, political minions, who will execute your agenda, reinforce your brand, and insulate yourself from political consequences. Authority is fragmented, roles are often undefined, and chaos becomes a management strategy. Like the Nazi bureaucracy's engineered disorder, Trump's second-term structure fosters internal competition, rhetorical warfare, and a political environment where improvisation often trumped planning.

As the Red Queen Theory suggests, the need to constantly evolve, to adapt to threats, stay ahead of rivals, and preserve one's position can ultimately destabilise the system itself. For the PRQ, survival is not about effective governance but about control, image, and influence. And for that, they require not just strategy, but an army of willing subordinates and manipulators to feed the chaos and followers to glorify the leader.

Trump's cabinet, especially in its second iteration, exemplifies this model. It is less a team of governing professionals and more a political ecosystem built for survival; chaotic, loyal, media-savvy, and always in motion.

However, what happens when personal ambition collides with moral uncertainty and rationalisations slip into denial or even delusion? When an individual's sense of right and wrong is drowned out by the shouting of a master who demands loyalty above all else?

Perhaps the costs of an amateur-run government can be blamed on others at first. Maybe it's a plane crash due to underqualified appointees, a contaminated supply chain that poisons baby formula, or thousands denied due process in the name of security. Perhaps veterans are left on the streets, or a once-eradicated childhood disease spirals out of control while the economy falters. All of it, some might argue, is a small price to pay for "government efficiency." Right?

Wrong. This isn't a reality television show; it's the management of a nation of over 345 million people, each with complex needs, histories, and identities. It should not be run by media personalities, wealthy insiders, or a clique of ideologues driven by religion, status, and self-interest. Governance demands expertise, empathy, and accountability, none of which should be optional in a functioning democracy and none of which should be entrusted to masters, manipulators, or minions.

Bibliography

Aaronson, T. (2019). *Trump's Pick for Top Intelligence Job Bragged of Experience as Terror Prosecutor — But He Doesn't Have Any*. The Intercept. https://theintercept.com/2019/07/30/john-ratcliffe-director-of-national-intelligence/

ABC News. (2015). *Marco Rubio: Cuban heritage, American dream*. Abc.net.au; ABC News. https://www.abc.net.au/news/2015-04-14/marco-rubio-cuban-heritage-american-dream-presidential-candidate/6390322

ABC News. (2025). *Tulsi Gabbard confirmed as United States' Director of National Intelligence*. Abc.net.au; ABC News. https://www.abc.net.au/news/2025-02-13/trump-names-tulsi-gabbard-director-of-national-intelligence/104930278

AFPI Names New Chair of Its China Policy Initiative. (2024). Americafirstpolicy.com. https://www.americafirstpolicy.com/issues/afpi-names-new-chair-of-its-china-policy-initiative

Ahmadi, A. A., & Debusmann Jr, B. (2025). Trump ousts national security adviser Mike Waltz. *BBC*. https://www.bbc.com/news/articles/cx20zw32lpgo

Ainsley, J., & Strickler, L. (2025). *Kristi Noem is Trump's pick to run DHS. But that doesn't mean she'd be in charge of one of its most important jobs*. NBC News. https://www.nbcnews.com/investigations/kristi-noem-trumps-pick-run-dhs-doesnt-mean-charge-one-important-jobs-rcna187639

Aleem, Z. (2023). *RFK Jr.'s independent bid is just strange enough to shake up 2024 in a big way*. MSNBC.com; MSNBC. https://www.msnbc.com/opinion/msnbc-opinion/robert-f-kennedy-jr-2024-independent-bid-rcna119227

Al Jazeera. (2025). *Why is Trump dismantling the Department of Education – and what's next?* Al Jazeera. https://www.aljazeera.com/news/2025/3/21/why-is-trump-dismantling-the-department-of-education-and-whats-next

Alexander, O. (2025). *Scott Turner (1972-)*. BlackPast.org. https://www.blackpast.org/african-american-history/scott-turner-1972/

American Immigration Council. (2024). *The Dream Act: An Overview*. American Immigration Council. https://www.americanimmigrationcouncil.org/research/dream-act-overview

Amy, J. (2025). *What to know about Doug Collins, Trump's pick to oversee veterans affairs*. NBC4 Washington. https://www.nbcwashington.com/news/national-international/doug-collins-veterans-affairs/3813381/

APM Reports. (2016). *APM Reports Documents*. Apmreports.org. https://features.apmreports.org/documents/?document=4421641-Minn-PAC-2016

Ashcraft, M. (2022). *Gov. Kristi Noem loves ranching, but God called her to a national stage | God Reports*. God Reports |. https://www.godreports.com/2022/07/gov-kristi-noem-loves-ranching-but-god-called-her-to-a-national-stage/

Ashcroft, J. (2004). *#07272004: Prepared Remarks of Attorney General John Ashcroft Holy Land Foundation Indictment*. Www.justice.gov. https://www.justice.gov/archive/ag/speeches/2004/72704ag.htm

Azhar, S. (2024). Prominent Wall Street boss Lutnick has been one of Trump's biggest cheerleaders. *Reuters*. https://www.reuters.com/world/us/prominent-wall-street-boss-lutnick-has-been-one-trumps-biggest-cheerleaders-2024-11-19/

Balkin Service. (2024). Dodik Doubles Down On Refusal To Join Sanctions Against Moscow In Meeting With Putin. *RadioFreeEurope/RadioLiberty*. https://www.rferl.org/a/serbia-dodik-refusal-sanctions-moscow-meeting-putin/32829529.html

Bardach, A. L. (2015). *Prodigal Son*. POLITICO Magazine. https://www.politico.com/magazine/story/2015/10/marco-rubio-profile-213275/

Barkley, S. (2024). *Former Southern Baptist pastor, chaplain selected to lead Veterans Administration*. IBSA News.

https://illinoisbaptist.org/former-southern-baptist-pastor-chaplain-selected-to-lead-veterans-administration/

Barstow, D., Craig, S., & Buettner, R. (2018). *Trump Engaged in Suspect Tax Schemes as He Reaped Riches From His Father*. The New York Times. https://www.nytimes.com/interactive/2018/10/02/us/politics/donald-trump-tax-schemes-fred-trump.html

BBC News. (2017). *Donald Trump's life story: From hotel developer to president*. BBC News. https://www.bbc.com/news/world-us-canada-35318432

Beggin, R. (2025). *How Speaker Mike Johnson's bond with Trump shapes GOP future*. USA TODAY. https://www.usatoday.com/story/news/politics/elections/2025/01/17/house-speaker-mike-johnson-relationship-trump-gop/77203452007/

Benen, S. (2022). *On asylum seekers, Marco Rubio flubs a test he should've passed*. MSNBC.com; MSNBC. https://www.msnbc.com/rachel-maddow-show/maddowblog/asylum-seekers-marco-rubio-flubs-test-ve-passed-rcna48926

Benen, S. (2025a). *"We feel betrayed": Venezuelans slam Trump for ending deportation protections*. MSNBC.com; MSNBC. https://www.msnbc.com/rachel-maddow-show/maddowblog/-feel-betrayed-venezuelans-slam-trump-ending-deportation-protections-rcna190831

Benen, S. (2025b). *Rubio taps Pete Marocco to run USAID, despite his Jan. 6 past*. MSNBC.com; MSNBC. https://www.msnbc.com/rachel-maddow-show/maddowblog/usaid-pete-marocco-jan-6-marco-rubio-rcna190610

Benen, S. (2025c). *Senior State Department official haunted by his scandalous record*. MSNBC.com; MSNBC. https://www.msnbc.com/rachel-maddow-show/maddowblog/senior-state-department-official-haunted-scandalous-record-rcna190647

Bessent, S. (2024). *SCOTT BESSENT: Let's talk tariffs. It's time to revitalize Alexander Hamilton's favorite tool*. Fox News.

https://www.foxnews.com/opinion/scott-bessent-talk-tariffs-its-time-revitalize-alexander-hamiltons-favorite-tool

Billionaires in Trump World | Revolving Door Project. (2025). Revolving Door Project. https://therevolvingdoorproject.org/billionaires-in-trump-world/

Biography | SENATOR RICK SCOTT. (2025). Www.rickscott.senate.gov. https://www.rickscott.senate.gov/biography

Bioguide Search. (2025). Bioguide.congress.gov. https://bioguide.congress.gov/search/bio/G000571

Birnbaum, M., Hudson, J., Davies, E., Ellison, S., & Allison, N. (2025). *Inside Waltz's ouster: Before Signalgate, talks with Israel angered Trump.* The Washington Post. https://www.washingtonpost.com/politics/2025/05/03/waltz-trump-israel/

Blake, S. (2025). *Kristi Noem Net Worth: DHS Secretary's Cash Raises Eyebrows.* Newsweek. https://www.newsweek.com/kristi-noem-net-worth-dhs-secretary-purse-raises-eyebrows-2062262

Bloomberg. (2024). *Rich, gay, and likes "friendshoring" — meet Scott Bessent, US' next Treasury Secy.* CNBCTV18. https://www.cnbctv18.com/world/who-is-scott-bessent-donald-trump-picks-us-treasury-secretary-profile-19513499.htm

Boiskin, A. (2025). *Trump's Treasury secretary nominee Scott Bessent '84 testifies before Senate Finance Committee.* Yale Daily News. https://yaledailynews.com/blog/2025/01/16/trumps-treasury-secretary-nominee-scott-bessent-84-testifies-before-senate-finance-committee/

Bomboy, S. (2023). *The Speaker of the House's Constitutional Role | Constitution Center.* National Constitution Center – Constitutioncenter.org. https://constitutioncenter.org/blog/the-speaker-of-the-houses-constitutional-role

Bond, S. (2023). *RFK Jr. is building a presidential campaign around conspiracy theories.* NPR. https://www.npr.org/2023/07/13/1187272781/rfk-jr-kennedy-conspiracy-theories-social-media-presidential-campaign

Booker, B. (2021). *WNBA Team Co-Owned By Ex-Sen. Kelly Loeffler Is Sold After Players' Criticism*. NPR. https://www.npr.org/2021/02/26/971877660/wnba-team-co-owned-by-ex-sen-kelly-loeffler-is-sold-after-players-criticism

Britni. (2020). *Kelly Loeffler: the WNBA owner against everything the league stands for*. The Guardian; The Guardian. https://www.theguardian.com/sport/2020/apr/07/kelly-loeffler-the-wnba-owner-against-everything-the-league-stands-for

Brod, R. (2025). *Trump administration profile: Howard Lutnick - OpenSecrets News*. OpenSecrets News. https://www.opensecrets.org/news/2025/03/trump-administration-profile-howard-lutnick

Brooke L. Rollins (2024) | Miller Center. (2025). Miller Center. https://millercenter.org/brooke-l-rollins-2024

Brooke Rollins Returns to TPPF as Senior Advisor, Roberts and Sindelar promoted - Texas Public Policy Foundation. (2021). *Texas Public Policy Foundation -*. https://www.texaspolicy.com/press/brooke-rollins-returns-to-tppf-as-senior-advisor-roberts-and-sindelar-promoted

Brooks, D. (2019). *In the House*. National Guard Association of the United States. https://www.ngaus.org/about-ngaus/newsroom/house

Brown, M., & McFetridge, S. (2025). *Brooke Rollins confirmed as Trump's agriculture secretary*. AP News. https://apnews.com/article/brooke-rollins-agriculture-disaster-aid-trade-wars-22b7de08daf0d9b0268e72ee3a8c9816

Canizales, A., & Kruse, M. (2023). *55 Things You Need to Know About Mike Johnson*. POLITICO. https://www.politico.com/news/magazine/2023/10/26/mike-johnson-house-speaker-55-things-to-know-00123593

Carney, J., & Guggenheim, B. (2025). *House Republicans huddle with Bessent on tax policy menu - Live Updates - POLITICO*. POLITICO; Politico. https://www.politico.com/live-updates/2025/03/10/congress/house-republicans-bessent-tax-policy-00222982

Carroll, K. (2025). *I worked in Trump's first administration. Here's why his team is using Signal*. The Guardian; The Guardian. https://www.theguardian.com/commentisfree/2025/apr/05/why-trump-administration-used-signal-hegseth-gabbard

Caselli, I. (2020). *Everybody was a child once. Remember that when they turn into your political foes (or worse)*. The Correspondent. https://thecorrespondent.com/709/everybody-was-a-child-once-remember-that-when-they-turn-into-your-political-foes-or-worse

CBS News Miami. (2024). *Who is Pam Bondi? Everything you need to know about Trump's new pick for attorney general*. Cbsnews.com. https://www.cbsnews.com/miami/news/what-to-know-about-pam-bondi-trumps-new-pick-for-attorney-general-2/

Children's Health Defense • Help Children's Health Defense and RFK, Jr. end the epidemic of poor health plaguing our children. (2019). Children's Health Defense; https://childrenshealthdefense.org/wp-content/themes/chd-theme/chd-theme. https://childrenshealthdefense.org/

Chris Wright. (2023). *Hart Energy*. https://www.hartenergy.com/agents-change/2023/chris-wright

Cleetus, R. (2025). *Russell Vought Is a Dangerous Choice to Head OMB. Congress Should Vote No on His Nomination*. The Equation. https://blog.ucs.org/rachel-cleetus/russell-vought-is-a-dangerous-choice-to-head-omb-congress-should-vote-no-on-his-nomination/

CNN Politics. (2015). *Donald Trump vs. Univision's Jorge Ramos*. CNN. https://edition.cnn.com/videos/politics/2015/08/26/donald-trump-jorge-ramos-argue-immigration-origwx-bw.cnn

Communications, F.I.U. (n.d.). *Marco Rubio*. Sipa.fiu.edu. https://sipa.fiu.edu/people/fellows/profiles/marcorubio.html

Contorno, S. (2024). *Trump's new chief of staff is an unassuming figure in his brash inner circle. She's also one of its most effective operators*. CNN. https://edition.cnn.com/2024/11/09/politics/susie-wiles-trump-chief-of-staff/index.html

Costa, J. L. (2024). *Taking flight: Karoline Leavitt's rise from Atkinson to the West Wing*. The Derry News. https://www.derrynews.com/news/local_news/taking-flight-karoline-leavitts-rise-from-atkinson-to-the-west-wing/article_410d653d-a296-5407-938b-5720b7d431c0.html

Cranston, M. (2024). *Trump tariffs: Can Donald Trump's trade representative Jamieson Greer win a war with China?* Australian Financial Review. https://www.afr.com/world/north-america/can-trump-s-new-trade-czar-win-a-war-with-china-20241129-p5kuh2

Daly, M. (2025). *Senate confirms fossil fuel CEO Chris Wright as energy secretary. He vows to "unleash" US resources.* AP News. https://apnews.com/article/trump-energy-wright-climate-nuclear-00e8e540be8b61498ca87740c327eb22

Daly, M., & Megerian, C. (2024). *Trump picks North Dakota Gov. Burgum to run Interior Dept. and new energy council.* PBS News. https://www.pbs.org/newshour/politics/trump-picks-north-dakota-gov-burgum-to-run-interior-dept-and-new-energy-council

Davis, S. (2023). *Speaker Johnson's close ties to Christian right — both mainstream and fringe.* NPR. https://www.npr.org/2023/11/15/1211536399/speaker-johnson-christian-nationalism-evangelical

Dayen, D. (2024). *When Pam Bondi Protected Foreclosure Fraudsters.* The American Prospect. https://prospect.org/justice/2024-11-22-when-pam-bondi-protected-foreclosure-fraudsters/

Detrow, S. (2025). *The political evolution of Secretary of State Marco Rubio.* NPR. https://www.npr.org/2025/03/08/nx-s1-5319063/the-political-evolution-of-secretary-of-state-marco-rubio

Devine, C., Tolan, C., Ash, A., & Lah, K. (2024). *Hidden-camera video shows Project 2025 co-author discussing his secret work preparing for a second Trump term.* CNN. https://edition.cnn.com/2024/08/15/politics/russ-vought-project-2025-trump-secret-recording-invs/index.html

Devine, M. (2022). *How Lee Zeldin's wife and two miracle daughters taught him how to defy the odds.* New York Post. https://nypost.com/2022/10/12/how-lee-zeldin-learned-he-can-defy-the-odds/

Department of Energy | Performance.gov. (2017). Obamaadministration.archives.performance.gov. https://obamaadministration.archives.performance.gov/agency/department-energy.html

Dickson, E. J. (2019). *QAnon Followers Think JFK Jr. Is Coming Back on the 4th of July*. Rolling Stone. https://www.rollingstone.com/culture/culture-features/qanon-jfk-jr-conspiracy-theory-854938/

Dilanian, K. (2025). *Pam Bondi reshapes the DOJ around Trump's priorities*. NBC News. https://www.nbcnews.com/politics/justice-department/s-trumps-justice-department-now-rcna195289

Dilanian, K. (2025a). *Kash Patel's new way of leading the FBI: Fewer morning intel briefings, more pro sports events*. NBC News. https://www.nbcnews.com/politics/national-security/kash-patels-new-way-leading-fbi-fewer-morning-intel-briefings-sports-e-rcna202865

Diongson, D. (2025). *Pam Bondi's net worth: From Florida prosecutor to U.S. Attorney General*. TheStreet. https://www.thestreet.com/personalities/pam-bondi-net-worth

Director of the CIA - CIA. (2025). Www.cia.gov. https://www.cia.gov/about/director-of-cia/

DNI Ratcliffe Welcomes U.S. Space Force as 18th Intelligence Community Member. (2021). United States Space Force. https://www.spaceforce.mil/News/Article/2467409/dni-ratcliffe-welcomes-us-space-force-as-18th-intelligence-community-member/

Donegan, M. (2023). *Mike Johnson, the new speaker of the House, is a gender extremist*. The Guardian; The Guardian. https://www.theguardian.com/commentisfree/2023/nov/08/mike-johnson-house-speaker-republican

Dorn, S. (2024). RFK Jr.'s Conspiracy Theories: Here's What Trump's Pick For Health Secretary Has Promoted. *Forbes*. https://www.forbes.com/sites/saradorn/2024/11/15/rfk-jrs-conspiracy-theories-heres-what-trumps-pick-for-health-secretary-has-promoted/

Doug Burgum. (2023). *North Dakota Office of the Governor*. https://www.governor.nd.gov/theodore-roosevelt-rough-rider-award/doug-burgum

Douglas A. Collins - U.S. Department of Veterans Affairs. (2025). U.S. Department of Veterans Affairs. https://department.va.gov/staff-biographies/douglas-a-collins/

Drusch, A., & Ordonez, F. (2018). *White House green-lights Texas think tank's ideas, irking Capitol Hill Republicans*. Fort Worth Star-Telegram. https://www.star-telegram.com/latest-news/article223205325.html

Duffy, S. (2024). *Senate Commerce Committee Nominee Questionnaire, 119th Congress* . Senate Service Files. https://www.commerce.senate.gov/services/files/A8C7499F-D2F5-42F2-A786-11A474C2ED90

Dunlap, D. W., & Perlez, J. (1985). NEW YORK DAY BY DAY; A Quiet Victory For Robert F. Kennedy Jr. *The New York Times*. https://www.nytimes.com/1985/06/04/nyregion/new-york-day-by-day-a-quiet-victory-for-robert-f-kennedy-jr.html

Durkee, A. (2025). Senate Confirms Kash Patel With 2 Republicans Opposing—What To Know About Trump's New FBI Director. *Forbes*. https://www.forbes.com/sites/alisondurkee/2025/02/20/senate-confirms-kash-patel-with-2-republicans-opposing-what-to-know-about-trumps-new-fbi-director/

Epler, P. (2024). *Tulsi Gabbard Through The Years: What A Long Strange Trip It's Been*. Honolulu Civil Beat. https://www.civilbeat.org/2024/12/tulsi-gabbard-through-the-years-what-a-long-strange-trip-its-been/

ERO EAD Thomas Homan receives 2015 Presidential Rank Award. (2024). Ice.gov. https://www.ice.gov/news/releases/ero-ead-thomas-homan-receives-2015-presidential-rank-award

ET Online. (2025a). *Who is Scott Bessent, Donald Trump's Treasury chief*. The Economic Times; Economic Times. https://economictimes.indiatimes.com/news/international/global-trends/who-is-scott-bessent-donald-trumps-treasury-chief/articleshow/118774885.cms

ET Online. (2025b). *Who is Pam Bondi, US Attorney General*. The Economic Times; Economic Times. https://economictimes.indiatimes.com/news/international/global-trends/who-is-pam-bondi-us-attorney-general/articleshow/118775180.cms?from=mdr

ET Online. (2025c). *Who is Lori Chavez-DeRemer, US Secretary of Labor*. The Economic Times; Economic Times. https://economictimes.indiatimes.com/news/international/global-trends/who-is-lori-chavez-deremer-us-secretary-of-labor/articleshow/118776704.cms?from=mdr

ET Online. (2025d). *Who is Doug Collins, US Veterans Affairs Secretary*. The Economic Times; Economic Times. https://economictimes.indiatimes.com/news/international/global-trends/who-is-doug-collins-us-veterans-affairs-secretary/articleshow/118776976.cms?from=mdr

ET Online. (2025e). *Who is Jamieson Greer, United States Trade Representative*. The Economic Times; Economic Times. https://economictimes.indiatimes.com/news/international/global-trends/jamieson-greer-united-states-trade-representative/articleshow/118741685.cms?from=mdr

Executive Associate Director, Enforcement and Removal Operations, Thomas Homan . (n.d.). House Documents. https://docs.house.gov/meetings/GO/GO06/20130627/101040/HHRG-113-GO06-Bio-HomanT-20130627.pdf

Family Research Council. (2025). *Marriage, Family, and Sexuality*. FRC. https://www.frc.org/family#gsc.tab=0

Find a Grave. (2020). Findagrave.com. https://www.findagrave.com/memorial/211213849/thurlow-bunyea-vought

Finnegan, W. (2019). *The Man Who Stood Up to Trump*. The New Yorker. https://www.newyorker.com/magazine/2015/10/05/the-man-who-wouldnt-sit-down

Frommer, F. (2025). *Pam Bondi | DOJ, Sanctuary Cities, & Facts*. Encyclopedia Britannica. https://www.britannica.com/biography/Pam-Bondi

Gabbard, T. (2025a). *SELECT COMMITTEE ON INTELLIGENCE UNITED STATES SENATE Additional Prehearing Questions for*. https://www.intelligence.senate.gov/sites/default/files/aphq-tgabbard-013025.pdf

Gabbard, T. (2025b). X (Formerly Twitter). https://x.com/DNIGabbard/status/1915150870255210774

Garrison, J. (2024). *The making of Doug Burgum: From small town North Dakota to Trump's possible VP*. USA TODAY. https://www.usatoday.com/story/news/politics/elections/2024/06/29/doug-burgum-north-dakota-vice-president/74049142007/

Guardian staff reporter. (2025). *"We will make mistakes": Musk pressed on claim $50m of condoms sent to Gaza – video*. The Guardian; The Guardian. https://www.theguardian.com/us-news/video/2025/feb/12/musk-says-he-will-make-mistakes-and-that-he-double-checks-with-trump-video

Gedeon, J. (2025). *Mike Johnson floats eliminating US courts as Trump faces judicial pressure*. The Guardian; The Guardian. https://www.theguardian.com/us-news/2025/mar/26/mike-johnson-congress-courts-trump

Gibson, K. (2025). *EPA to review landmark 2009 finding that greenhouse gases are a danger to public health*. Cbsnews.com; CBS News. https://www.cbsnews.com/news/epa-greenhouse-gases-endangerment-finding-public-health-trump/

Goldberg, J. (2025). *The Atlantic*. The Atlantic; theatlantic. https://www.theatlantic.com/politics/archive/2025/03/trump-administration-accidentally-texted-me-its-war-plans/682151/?gift=kPTlqn0J1iP9IBZcsdI5IVJpB2t9BYyxpzU4sooa69M&utm_source=copy-link&utm_medium=social&utm_campaign=share

Golinger, J. (2024). *Meet Susie Wiles' Controversial Corporate Lobbying Clients - Public Citizen*. Public Citizen.

https://www.citizen.org/article/meet-susie-wiles-controversial-corporate-lobbying-clients/

Gordon, M. (2011). *Mary Ellen Mark*. Maryellenmark.com. https://www.maryellenmark.com/bibliography/magazines/article/new-york/howard-lutnicks-second-life-637516783238293151/N

Goss, A. (2024). *Tall tale about little dictator forces amendments to Noem's book*. Thedakotascout.com; The Dakota Scout. https://www.thedakotascout.com/p/tall-tale-about-little-dictator-forces

Goss, A., & Ellis, J. (2024). *Gov. Kristi Noem's account of meeting North Korean dictator in doubt*. Thedakotascout.com; The Dakota Scout. https://www.thedakotascout.com/p/gov-kristi-noems-account-of-meeting

Gov-Elect Burgum announces marriage. (2016). *KX NEWS*. https://www.kxnet.com/news/gov-elect-burgum-announces-marriage/

GPAHE. (2024). *Kristi Noem, Trump Nominee for Secretary of the Department of Homeland Security*. Global Project against Hate and Extremism. https://globalextremism.org/post/kristi-noem/

Gramlich, J. (2021). *How Trump compares with other recent presidents in appointing federal judges*. Pew Research Center; Pew Research Center. https://www.pewresearch.org/short-reads/2021/01/13/how-trump-compares-with-other-recent-presidents-in-appointing-federal-judges/

Gregorian, D. (2023). *GOP presidential candidate Burgum says he wouldn't do business with Trump*. NBC News. https://www.nbcnews.com/politics/2024-election/gop-presidential-candidate-burgum-says-wouldnt-business-trump-rcna93167

Griffiths, B. D. (2023). *RFK Jr. and Cheryl Hines' net worth is $15 million*. Business Insider. https://www.businessinsider.com/robert-kennedy-jr-net-worth-cheryl-hines-15-million-2023-8

Guardian staff reporter. (2025). *Marco Rubio says South Africa's ambassador to US is "no longer welcome."* The Guardian; The Guardian.

https://www.theguardian.com/world/2025/mar/15/south-africa-ambassador-us-no-longer-welcome-marco-rubio-ebrahim-rasool

Gupta, K. (2024). *Howard Lutnick '83 is Shaping the Trump White House*. The Clerk. https://haverfordclerk.com/howard-lutnick-83-is-shaping-the-trump-white-house/

Heckman, J. (2025). *SBA to cut 43% of workforce, return to pre-pandemic staffing levels*. Federal News Network - Helping Feds Meet Their Mission.; Federal News Network. https://federalnewsnetwork.com/workforce/2025/03/sba-to-cut-43-of-workforce-return-to-pre-pandemic-staffing-levels/

Hegseth, P. (2020). *American Crusade*. Center Street.

Hegseth, P. (2024). *The War on Warriors*. HarperCollins.

Hilburn, G. (2023). *New House Speaker Mike Johnson of Louisiana was trusted member of Trump inner circle*. The Times. https://www.shreveporttimes.com/story/news/2023/10/24/louisiana-rep-mike-johnson-was-trusted-member-of-trump-inner-circle-and-now-running-for-speaker/71304607007/

Hill, M. L., & McGraw, M. (2024). *Trump taps loyalist Rollins for USDA chief in surprise pick - POLITICO*. POLITICO; Politico. https://www.politico.com/news/2024/11/23/trump-loyalist-brooke-rollins-usda-secretary-surprise-nomination-00191391

Hornbeck, D. (2025). *What does the education secretary do?* PBS News. https://www.pbs.org/newshour/politics/what-does-the-education-secretary-do

Houghtaling, E. Q. (2023). *Here's the Story of How Mike Johnson Became Too Right-Wing for His Own Father*. The New Republic. https://newrepublic.com/post/177533/mike-johnson-stepmom-extremist-religious-beliefs-alienated-father-toxic-burn-pits

Hsu, S. S., Joselow, M., & Rivero, N. (2025). *FBI takes up EPA probe amid pushback from judge, prosecutors*. The Washington Post. https://www.washingtonpost.com/dc-md-va/2025/02/27/trump-fbi-epa-grant-investigation/

Huang, C., & Rolfes, E. (2012). *Meet the Incoming Congressional Class Veterans*. Archive.org. https://web.archive.org/web/20140118170840/http://www.pbs.org

/newshour/rundown/2012/11/meet-the-incoming-congressional-class-veterans.html

Hubbard, K. (2025). *EPA administrator Lee Zeldin says Trump deregulatory actions won't have adverse effects on people and the environment.* Cbsnews.com; CBS News. https://www.cbsnews.com/news/lee-zeldin-epa-administrator-trump-environmental-deregulations/

Ivermectin (Oral Route) Description and Brand Names - Mayo Clinic. (n.d.). Www.mayoclinic.org. https://www.mayoclinic.org/drugs-supplements/ivermectin-oral-route/description/drg-20064397

Jaffa, J. (2025). *Who is Howard Lutnick, the "abandoned" orphan with the fate of the global economy in his hands?* The Jewish Chronicle. https://www.thejc.com/news/usa/howard-lutnick-abandoned-orphan-tariffs-commerce-bnjfrjgo

John Ratcliffe. (2019). The Heritage Foundation. https://www.heritage.org/staff/john-ratcliffe

John Ratcliffe. (2025). John Ratcliffe. https://john-ratcliffe.com/about/

John Ratcliffe - The Ashcroft Group. (2014). Archive.org. https://web.archive.org/web/20140529085010/http://www.ashcroftgroupllc.com/ourteam/john-ratcliffe/

John, A. S. (2025). *Things to know about the Trump administration order on miles per gallon for cars and pickups.* AP News. https://apnews.com/article/climate-trump-mpg-fuel-economy-standards-automakers-0ef9147a0c3874a50a194e439f604261

Johnson, C. (2025). *Kristi Noem largely glides unnoticed amid other Trump picks - Roll Call.* Roll Call. https://rollcall.com/2025/01/14/kristi-noem-largely-glides-unnoticed-amid-other-trump-picks/

Joselow, M. (2025). *EPA chief says Biden was "irresponsibly shoveling boatloads of cash," vows to get back $20 billion.* Washington Post; The Washington Post. https://www.washingtonpost.com/climate-environment/2025/02/12/lee-zeldin-epa-climate-funding/

Joseph, C. (2022). *Trump-Endorsed Candidate JD Vance Once Said Trump Might Be "America's Hitler."* VICE. https://www.vice.com/en/article/jd-vance-trump-messages/

Khan, M. (2025). *Karoline Leavitt, press secretary from NH, addresses "atypical" 32-year age gap with husband.* Portsmouth Herald.

https://www.seacoastonline.com/story/news/politics/2025/03/19/karoline-leavitt-press-secretary-nh-husband-age-gap/82538174007/

Kelefa Sanneh. (2017). *What Does Tulsi Gabbard Believe?* The New Yorker. https://www.newyorker.com/magazine/2017/11/06/what-does-tulsi-gabbard-believe

Kight, S. W. (2017). *The big $$$ donors to Trump's Inaugural Committee.* Axios. https://www.axios.com/2017/12/15/the-big-donors-to-trumps-inaugural-committee-1513301711

Kim, E. T. (2025). *Lori Chavez-DeRemer, Donald Trump's Pro-Union Labor Secretary.* The New Yorker. https://www.newyorker.com/news/the-lede/lori-chavez-deremer-donald-trumps-pro-union-labor-secretary

Kim, S. R. (2025). *Former Democrat Tulsi Gabbard raked in massive income engaging Republican audience, filing shows.* ABC News. https://abcnews.go.com/Politics/tulsi-gabbard-income-disclosure-wealth/story?id=117891226

Kim, S. R., & Lalee Ibssa. (2024). *Trump brings in more than $6.8 million from Greenville, South Carolina, fundraiser ahead of primary.* ABC News. https://abcnews.go.com/Politics/trump-brings-68-million-greenville-fundraiser/story?id=107397720

Kime, P., & Kheel, R. (2024). *Who Is Doug Collins? A Look at Trump's Pick to Head the VA.* Military.com. https://www.military.com/daily-news/2024/11/15/who-doug-collins-look-trumps-pick-head-va.html

Kinnard, M. (2024). *What to know about Pete Hegseth, Trump's defense secretary pick.* AP News. https://apnews.com/article/who-is-pete-hegseth-trump-defense-secretary-2e2bdd16c8e90f5d037f763cfadbde94

Kreps, D. (2023). *Mike Johnson Admits He and His Son Monitor Each Other's Porn Intake.* Rolling Stone. https://www.rollingstone.com/politics/politics-news/mike-johnson-son-monitor-porn-intake-covenant-eyes-1234870634/

Kristi Noem. (2025). *National Governors Association.* https://www.nga.org/governor/kristi-noem/

Kruse, M. (2024). *The Most Feared and Least Known Political Operative in America*. POLITICO; Politico. https://www.politico.com/news/magazine/2024/04/26/susie-wiles-trump-desantis-profile-00149654

Kullgren, I. (2024). *Labor Nominee Wields Personal Touch to Win Over Unions and Trump*. @BLaw. https://news.bloomberglaw.com/daily-labor-report/trump-labor-nominee-charted-unlikely-path-from-mayor-to-cabinet

Kuo, J. (2023). *Speaker Mike Johnson's Past Holds Many Unanswered Questions*. Substack.com; The Status Kuo. https://statuskuo.substack.com/p/speaker-mike-johnsons-past-holds

Lakritz, T., & Griffiths, B. D. (2025). *Who is RFK Jr.? All about his family, controversies, political career*. Business Insider. https://www.businessinsider.com/robert-f-kennedy-rfk-jr

Lawder, D., & Jackson, K. (2024). Trump picks loyalist Navarro to reprise White House trade role. *Reuters*. https://www.reuters.com/world/us/trump-picks-navarro-be-senior-counselor-trade-manufacturing-2024-12-04/

Lawrence, Q. (2025). *Doug Collins, Trump's nominee to lead the VA, vows to work across the aisle to help vets*. NPR. https://www.npr.org/2025/01/22/nx-s1-5269946/doug-collins-trump-veterans-affairs

Lefebvre, B. (2025). *Trump's economic tumult tests the oil industry's patience*. POLITICO; Politico. https://www.politico.com/news/2025/04/14/trumps-economic-tumult-tests-the-oil-industrys-patience-00287408

Leingang, R. (2024). *Project 2025: the Trump picks with ties to ultra-rightwing policy manifesto*. The Guardian; The Guardian. https://www.theguardian.com/us-news/2024/nov/22/project-2025-trump-picks

Letter to Vote No on the Confirmation of Eric Scott Turner as Secretary of Housing and Urban Development. (2025). *Southern Poverty Law Center*. https://www.splcenter.org/resources/policies/letter-vote-no-eric-scott-turner-secretary-housing-urban-development/

LeVine, M., & Arkin, J. (2020). *Kelly Loeffler embraces her wealth — and private jet — to jump-start campaign*. POLITICO; Politico. https://www.politico.com/news/2020/05/06/kelly-loeffler-campaign-236134

Licon, A. G. (2024). *What to know about Scott Turner, Trump's pick for housing secretary*. AP News. https://apnews.com/article/housing-secretary-trump-scott-turner-nfl-727417b56d0e1f85a40eaf5f7d13d42f

Life and money management. (2015). *Yalealumnimagazine.com*, Sept/Oct 2015. https://doi.org/1091102/halfpage_300x600

Linda McMahon. (2024). *OpenSecrets*. https://www.opensecrets.org/revolving-door/linda-mcmahon/summary?id=81848

Lindenmayer, D. (2024). *The Forest Wars* (First Edition). Allen & Unwin.

Livingston, A. (2020). *President Donald Trump's impeachment advisory team includes John Ratcliffe*. The Texas Tribune. https://www.texastribune.org/2020/01/20/president-donald-trump-texas-rep-john-ratcliffe-impeachment-advisor/

Liy, M. V. (2025). *Marco Rubio cements his position as Trump's trusted point man on foreign policy*. EL PAÍS English. https://english.elpais.com/usa/2025-05-05/marco-rubio-cements-his-position-as-trumps-trusted-point-man-on-foreign-policy.html

Lockhart, B. (2010). *McMahons' bankruptcy a murky chapter in her rags-to-riches tale*. Connecticut Post. https://www.ctpost.com/local/article/mcmahons-bankruptcy-a-murky-chapter-in-her-682114.php

Lori Chavez-DeRemer, the incumbent Republican candidate for Oregon's 5th Congressional District, on abortion, Israel and immigration. (2024). Opb. https://www.opb.org/article/2024/10/18/lori-chavez-deremer-republican-candidate-oregon-5th-congressional-district/

Lowell, H. (2022). *Top Trump adviser granted immunity testifies in Mar-a-Lago papers case*. The Guardian; The Guardian. https://www.theguardian.com/us-news/2022/nov/04/trump-adviser-immunity-mar-a-lago-papers-kash-patel

Ma, J. (2025). *Trump's pick for Treasury secretary discloses assets worth at least $521 million, including a home in the Bahamas and S&P 500 ETFs*. Fortune. https://fortune.com/2025/01/12/scott-bessent-net-worth-trump-treasury-secretary-nominee-personal-assets-financial-disclosure/

MacKinnon, A., & Bazail-Eimil, E. (2025). *Ratcliffe the good MAGA foot soldier*. POLITICO. https://www.politico.com/newsletters/national-security-daily/2025/03/31/ratcliffe-the-good-maga-foot-soldier-00260771

Mannes, A. (2024). *J.D. Vance and the Model of the Modern Vice Presidency*. Lawfare. https://www.lawfaremedia.org/article/j.d.-vance-and-the-model-of-the-modern-vice-presidency

Mathur-Ashton, A. (2024). *What to Know About Chris Wright, Trump's Pick for Energy Secretary*. US News & World Report; U.S. News & World Report. https://www.usnews.com/news/national-news/articles/2024-11-18/who-is-chris-wright-trumps-pick-for-energy-secretary

Mattie, A. (2025). *Health and Human Services secretary influences every aspect of America's health*. The Conversation. https://theconversation.com/health-and-human-services-secretary-influences-every-aspect-of-americas-health-245983

Matza, M. (2024). Susie Wiles: Who is Trump's new chief of staff? *BBC*. https://www.bbc.com/news/articles/cd0gdnp9d3ko

McAdams, D. P. (2016). *A Psychologist Analyzes Donald Trump's Personality*. The Atlantic; The Atlantic. https://www.theatlantic.com/magazine/archive/2016/06/the-mind-of-donald-trump/480771/

McArthur, T. (2024). *Howard Lutnick*. IMDb. https://www.imdb.com/name/nm2965714/bio/

McCaskill, N, & Dawsey, J. (2017). *Bannon out as White House chief strategist*. POLITICO. https://web.archive.org/web/20170818195927/http://www.politico.com/story/2017/08/18/bannon-out-as-white-house-chief-strategist-241786

McCausland, P., & Halpert, M. (2024). *Pete Hegseth: Trump defence pick surprises Washington, here's why*. BBC. https://www.bbc.com/news/articles/c04lvv6ee3lo

McCormack, K., & Gissen, L. (2025). *Who is Pam Bondi's husband John Wakefield? Inside Trump's new attorney general's turbulent love life*. Mail Online; Daily Mail. https://www.dailymail.co.uk/femail/article-14364827/trump-attorney-general-pam-bondi-husband-john-wakefield-marriage-divorce.html

McCormick, M. (2024). *Donald Trump: How oil "wildcatters" such as Harold Hamm, Doug Burgum and Chris Wright seized the US energy agenda*. Australian Financial Review. https://www.afr.com/world/north-america/how-oil-wildcatters-seized-trump-s-energy-agenda-20241120-p5ks93

McGraw, M. (2024). *"One Handsome Son-of-a-Bitch": How Donald Trump Fell for J.D. Vance - POLITICO*. POLITICO; Politico. https://www.politico.com/news/magazine/2024/07/16/donald-trump-jd-vance-relationship-00168422

Megyn Kelly. (2024). *Pete Hegseth Speaks Out, On Media Smears, Responding to Accusations, and How He'd Reform Military*. YouTube. https://www.youtube.com/watch?v=IjHk96-UCrE

Mehta, J. (2025). *Linda McMahon led WWE and the SBA. The U.S. Education Dept. may be next*. NPR. https://www.npr.org/2025/02/08/nx-s1-5251642/linda-mcmahon-trump-wwe-education-secretary-nominee

Mentzer, R. (2019). *Duffy's Resignation In Trump Country Has Both Parties Readying For Battle*. WPR. https://www.wpr.org/politics/duffys-resignation-trump-country-has-both-parties-readying-battle

Messerly, M., Allison, N., McGraw, M., & Fuchs, H. (2024). *5 things you need to know about Susie Wiles - POLITICO*. POLITICO; Politico. https://www.politico.com/news/2024/11/07/5-things-you-need-to-know-about-susie-wiles-00188391

Metzger, B. (2025). *Trump FBI pick Kash Patel made more than $2.6 million last year*. Business Insider.

https://www.businessinsider.com/trump-fbi-director-kash-patel-financial-disclosure-2025-1

Michael Waltz. (2025). *Jewishvirtuallibrary.org*. https://www.jewishvirtuallibrary.org/michael-waltz

Mike Waltz's net worth revealed. (2024). Finbold. https://finbold.com/guide/mike-waltz-net-worth-revealed/

Mimbela, R. (2025). *Trump's attack on the department of education, explained*. American Civil Liberties Union. https://www.aclu.org/news/racial-justice/trumps-attack-on-the-department-of-education-explained

MSN. (2025). Msn.com. https://www.msn.com/en-in/news/world/kash-patel-education-qualification-from-law-school-grad-to-trump-s-intelligence-visionary/ar-BB1rdMqv

Mueller, J. (2024). *5 things to know about Trump Agriculture pick Brooke Rollins*. The Hill. https://thehill.com/homenews/administration/5008075-brooke-rollins-agriculture-trump-what-to-know/

Murphy, B., & Barry-Jester, A. (2025). *Trump Official Destroying USAID Secretly Met With Christian Nationalists Abroad in Defiance of U.S. Policy*. ProPublica. https://www.propublica.org/article/usaid-peter-marocco-state-department-bosnia-serbia-diplomacy-trump-foreign-policy

Murray, I., & Osborne, M. (2022). *Tulsi Gabbard announces she is leaving Democratic Party, calling it an "elitist cabal of warmongers."* ABC News. https://abcnews.go.com/Politics/tulsi-gabbard-announces-leaving-democratic-party/story?id=91326164

Murray, R. (2020). *Kelly Loeffler*. GLAAD | GLAAD Rewrites the Script for LGBTQ Acceptance.; GLAAD. https://glaad.org/gap/kelly-loeffler/

NASA. (2024). *Evidence*. Science.nasa.gov; NASA. https://science.nasa.gov/climate-change/evidence/

Nast, C. (2016). *Robert F. Kennedy Jr. on the Environment, Election, and a "Dangerous" Donald Trump*. Vanity Fair. https://www.vanityfair.com/news/2016/08/robert-f-kennedy-jr-on-the-environment-election-and-donald-trump

National Security Adviser Mike Walz. (2024). American Bridge PAC. https://www.americanbridgepac.org/trumps-orbit/trumps-potential-administration-officials/mike-waltz/

Natter, A., Wethe, D., & Crowley, K. (2024). *Energy CEO Who Drank Fracking Fluid Is Now Trump's Oil Evangelist.* Financialpost; Financial Post. https://financialpost.com/pmn/business-pmn/energy-ceo-who-drank-fracking-fluid-is-now-trumps-oil-evangelist

Nazaryan, A. (2025). *Lee Zeldin's EPA deregulation comments remind us we'll all feel Trump administration effects soon.* MSNBC.com; MSNBC. https://www.msnbc.com/opinion/msnbc-opinion/lee-zeldin-epa-deregulation-trump-administration-climate-effects-rcna202489

Neschis, M. (2025). *Inside Karoline Leavitt's past life as college athlete before White House role.* Irish Star. https://www.irishstar.com/sport/other-sports/caroline-leavitt-saint-anselm-college-34827415

Net worth, bio and insider trades. (2024). *Benzinga.* https://www.benzinga.com/sec/insider-trades/0001292100/

Noah, T. (2025). *Everybody Hates Howard Lutnick. The New Republic.* https://newrepublic.com/article/193710/howard-lutnick-trump-tariff-economy

Noem, Kristi | US House of Representatives: History, Art & Archives. (2025). History.house.gov. https://history.house.gov/People/Detail/19064

Office of the Attorney General. (2022). *Justice.gov.* https://www.justice.gov/doj/organization-mission-and-functions-manual-office-attorney-general

OFFICE OF THE U.S. TRADE REPRESENTATIVE (USTR) | U.S. Department of the Interior. (2015). Www.doi.gov. https://www.doi.gov/invasivespecies/ustr

Office of the United States Trade Representative. (2020). *Phase One | United States Trade Representative.* Ustr.gov. https://ustr.gov/phase-one

Office, U. E. (2025). *U.S. Trustee Program/Dept. of Justice*. Justice.gov. https://www.justice.gov/ust/eo/bapcpa/20250401/bci_data/median_income_table.htm

Ortiz, M. (2024). *The trailblazing political and Army career of Tulsi Gabbard*. Yahoo News. https://www.yahoo.com/news/trailblazing-political-army-career-tulsi-191604107.html

Palmer, D., & Desrochers, D. (2025). *Senate confirms Jamieson Greer to be US trade representative - Live Updates - POLITICO*. POLITICO; Politico. https://www.politico.com/live-updates/2025/02/26/congress/senate-confirms-jamieson-greer-to-be-u-s-trade-representative-00206232

Perry, H., & Daugherty, E. (2025). *What Was Defense Secretary Nominee Pete Hegseth '03 Like at Princeton?* Princeton Alumni Weekly. https://paw.princeton.edu/article/what-was-defense-secretary-nominee-pete-hegseth-03-princeton

Perry, R. (2024). *Opinion: Brooke Rollins: Texas' next world changer*. Agri-Pulse.com; Agri-Pulse Communications, Inc. https://www.agri-pulse.com/articles/22083-opinion-brooke-rollins-texas-next-world-changer

Piwowarski, M. (2025). *Doug Burgum Net Worth: From Small-Town Roots to Tech Mogul and Political Leader - Chemical City Paper*. Chemical City Paper. https://chemicalcitypaper.com/doug-burgum-net-worth-from-small-town-roots-to-tech-mogul-and-political-leader/

Planas, R. (2018, April 13). *Trump Hired A Cop To Run ICE. It Didn't Work Out*. HuffPost. https://www.huffpost.com/entry/thomas-homan-trump-ice-director_n_5acbae94e4b09d0a11964dc4

Pontes, M. (2023). *Karoline Leavitt Speaks with Students at NHIOP*. Anselm.edu. https://www.anselm.edu/about/anselmian-hub/news/karoline-leavitt-speaks-students-nhiop

Pope Francis. (2025). *Letter of the Holy Father to the Bishops of the United States of America (10 February 2025) | Francis*. Vatican.va. https://www.vatican.va/content/francesco/en/letters/2025/documents/20250210-lettera-vescovi-usa.html

Rappeport, A., & Haberman, M. (2024). Trump Taps Investor Scott Bessent as Treasury Secretary. *The New York Times*.

https://www.nytimes.com/2024/11/22/business/trump-scott-bessent-treasury.html

Ratcliffe for Congress» John's Story. (2013). Archive.org. https://web.archive.org/web/20131213150058/http://ratcliffeforcongress.com/johns-story/

Rathore, B. (2025). *Mike Waltz family: All about his wife Julia Nesheiwat and his children*. Hindustan Times. https://www.hindustantimes.com/world-news/us-news/mike-waltz-family-all-about-his-wife-julia-nesheiwat-and-his-children-101746113972812.html

Redden, M., & Kroll, A. (2024). *"Put Them in Trauma": Inside a Key MAGA Leader's Plans for a New Trump Agenda*. ProPublica. https://www.propublica.org/article/video-donald-trump-russ-vought-center-renewing-america-maga

Rep.-elect Lee Zeldin (R-N.Y.-01). (2025). TheHill. https://web.archive.org/web/20141128000011/http://thehill.com/new-members-guide-2014/223737-rep-elect-lee-zeldin-r-ny-01

Reuters. (2020). *Factbox: Donald Trump's legacy - six policy takeaways*. Reuters. https://www.reuters.com/article/world/factbox-donald-trumps-legacy-six-policy-takeaways-idUSKBN27F1GH/

Reuters. (2023). FACTBOX Who is Mike Johnson, the new Republican US House Speaker? *Reuters*. https://www.reuters.com/world/us/who-is-mike-johnson-new-republican-us-house-speaker-2023-10-25/

Reynoso, R. (2023). *The missing years from Speaker Mike Johnson's biography*. Faith on View. https://www.faithonview.com/the-missing-years-from-speaker-mike-johnsons-biography/

Roe v. Wade: *410 U.S. 113. (1973) Justia US Supreme Court Center*. (1973). Perma.cc. https://perma.cc/Q9DZ-6L3V

Rose, J. (2025). *Trump's Cabinet pick for secretary of transportation is Sean Duffy. Here's what to know*. NPR. https://www.npr.org/2025/01/15/nx-s1-5261017/sean-duffy-transportation-secretary-dot-confirmation

Russ Vought - Office of Management and Budget (Feb. 2025-), Director Nominee - Biography | LegiStorm. (2025). Legistorm.com.

https://www.legistorm.com/person/bio/11259/Russell_Thurlow_V ought.html

Saric, I. (2025). *Who is Russ Vought, Trump's pick for DC's regulatory gatekeeper*. Axios. https://www.axios.com/2025/01/29/russ-vought-omb-trump

Sarkar, I. (2025). *South China Morning Post*. South China Morning Post. https://www.scmp.com/magazines/style/entertainment/article/3299563/meet-family-donald-trumps-border-tsar-tom-homan-and-what-did-his-wife-former-american-airlines

Saul, D. (2025). What To Know About Scott Bessent: Treasury Pick Will Tout Trump "Economic Golden Age" In Confirmation Hearing. *Forbes*. https://www.forbes.com/sites/dereksaul/2025/01/16/what-to-know-about-scott-bessent-treasury-pick-will-tout-trump-economic-golden-age-in-confirmation-hearing/

Scahill, J. (2024). *Tulsi Gabbard Would Be a Shock to the U.S. Intelligence System*. Dropsitenews.com; Drop Site News. https://www.dropsitenews.com/p/tulsi-gabbard-record-director-national-intelligence

Scheck, T. (2018). *Words and deeds out of alignment for potential Cabinet appointment and Fox News personality*. Apmreports.org; APM Reports. https://www.apmreports.org/story/2018/03/27/pete-hegseth-potential-cabinet-appointment

Sean Duffy | Bipartisan Policy Center. (2024). Bipartisanpolicy.org. https://bipartisanpolicy.org/person/sean-duffy/

Secretary Doug Burgum | U.S. Department of the Interior. (2025). U.S. Department of the Interior. https://www.doi.gov/secretary-doug-burgum

Securities Docket. (2009). *Former U.S. Attorneys Johnny Sutton and John Ratcliffe Join New Ashcroft Law Firm - Securities Docket*. Securities Docket. https://www.securitiesdocket.com/2009/04/22/former-us-attorneys-johnny-sutton-and-john-ratcliffe-join-new-ashcroft-law-firm/

Segers, G. (2018). *Trump says he finished the written answers for Mueller investigation*. Cbsnews.com; CBS News.

https://www.cbsnews.com/news/trump-heads-to-mar-a-lago-for-thanksgiving-holiday-2018-11-20-live-updates/

Segers, G. (2018b). *Tulsi Gabbard on Twitter: Calls Trump "Saudi Arabia's bitch"; says that's not "America First."* Cbsnews.com; CBS News. https://www.cbsnews.com/news/tulsi-gabbard-tweet-says-trump-is-saudi-arabias-bitch-twitter-wednesday/

Sen, M. (2025). *Why federal courts are unlikely to save democracy from Trump's and Musk's attacks*. The Conversation. https://theconversation.com/why-federal-courts-are-unlikely-to-save-democracy-from-trumps-and-musks-attacks-249533

Senior, J. (2016). Review: *In "Hillbilly Elegy," a Tough Love Analysis of the Poor Who Back Trump*. The New York Times. https://www.nytimes.com/2016/08/11/books/review-in-hillbilly-elegy-a-compassionate-analysis-of-the-poor-who-love-trump.html

Shafiq, S., & Encinas, A. (2025). *Who is Sean Duffy? Transportation secretary nominee met wife on "Real World."* USA TODAY. https://www.usatoday.com/story/news/politics/elections/2025/01/16/who-is-sean-duffy-transportation-secretary-nominee-real-world/77721260007/

Silliman, D. (2024). *Died: Disgraced Southern Baptist Leader Paul Pressler - Christianity Today*. Christianity Today. https://www.christianitytoday.com/2024/06/paul-pressler-dead-disgrace-sbc-conservative-resurgence/

Small Business Administration. (2015). *About SBA | The U.S. Small Business Administration | SBA.gov*. Sba.gov. https://www.sba.gov/about-sba

Smith, S. B. (2024). *The Close Relationship Between Donald Trump's Nominee for Treasury Secretary and the Royal Family*. Substack.com; ROYALS EXTRA BY SALLY BEDELL SMITH. https://sallybedellsmith.substack.com/p/the-close-relationship-between-donald

Spivak, J. (2024). *Why Marco Rubio probably won't ever be president*. The Hill. https://thehill.com/opinion/campaign/4998958-why-secretary-of-state-rubio-likely-wont-ever-be-president-rubio/

Springer, P. (2023). *His grandmother saw Sitting Bull. His great-grandmother clashed with Custer. Gov. Burgum's deep Dakota roots.* Grand Forks Herald. https://www.grandforksherald.com/news/north-dakota/his-grandmother-saw-sitting-bull-his-great-grandmother-clashed-with-custer-gov-burgums-deep-dakota-roots

Srinivasan, H. (2025). *Kash Patel Net Worth: Here's How Trump's FBI Director Made His Money.* Investopedia. https://www.investopedia.com/kash-patel-net-worth-here-s-how-trump-s-fbi-director-made-his-money-11687334

Staff Members | Vought Strategies. (2025). Archive.md. https://archive.md/2025.02.11-212329/https://voughtstrategies.com/staff/#selection-265.13-265.115

Statement by Secretary Granholm on the President's Fiscal Year 2025 Budget. (2024). Energy.gov. https://www.energy.gov/articles/statement-secretary-granholm-presidents-fiscal-year-2025-budget

Statement from Secretary Kelly on the President's Appointment of Thomas D. Homan as Acting ICE Director | Homeland Security. (2024). U.S. Department of Homeland Security. https://www.dhs.gov/archive/news/2017/01/30/statement-secretary-kelly-presidents-appointment-thomas-d-homan-acting-ice-director

Steffen, S. (2024). *Who is Lee Zeldin, Trump's pick as new EPA head?* Dw.com; Deutsche Welle. https://www.dw.com/en/new-trump-administration-zeldin-in-charge-of-environmental-protection-all-you-need-to-know/a-70773017

Storr, W. (2021). *The status game.* William Collins.

Suozzo, A. (2013). *Community Engagement And Opportunity Council, Full Filing - Nonprofit Explorer - ProPublica.* ProPublica. https://projects.propublica.org/nonprofits/organizations/862595346/202303199349330190/full

Supreme Court of the United States. (2023). https://www.supremecourt.gov/opinions/22pdf/21-476_c185.pdf

Swan, J. (2016). *Bannon set up Trump-Gabbard meeting*. The Hill. https://thehill.com/homenews/administration/307106-bannon-set-up-trump-gabbard-meeting/

Swartsell, N. (2014). *John Ratcliffe touts time as U.S. attorney in run against U.S. Rep. Ralph Hall...* Dallas News. https://web.archive.org/web/20170130081422/https://www.dallasnews.com/news/local-politics/2014/04/04/john-ratcliffe-touts-time-as-u.s.-attorney-in-run-against-u.s.-rep.-ralph-hall

Tait, R. (2024). *Trump reportedly picks Kristi Noem to run homeland security department*. The Guardian; The Guardian. https://www.theguardian.com/us-news/2024/nov/12/kristi-noem-homeland-security-donald-trump

Tait, R. (2024b). *Who is Tulsi Gabbard, Trump's pick for director of national intelligence?* The Guardian; The Guardian. https://www.theguardian.com/us-news/2024/nov/14/trump-tulsi-gabbard-national-intelligence

Tan, S. (2025). *How Many Wives and Children Does Pete Hegseth Have?* International Business Times UK. https://www.ibtimes.co.uk/how-many-wives-children-does-pete-hegseth-have-1730156

Teamsters. (n.d.). *Who Are The Teamsters?* International Brotherhood of Teamsters. https://teamster.org/about/who-are-teamsters/

Texas Legislature Online - 83(R) Text for HB 3350. (2013). *Texas.gov*. https://capitol.texas.gov/billlookup/Text.aspx?LegSess=83R&Bill=HB3350

Texas Legislature Online - 83(R) History for HB 1888. (2013). *Texas.gov*. https://capitol.texas.gov/billlookup/History.aspx?LegSess=83R&Bill=HB1888

Texas Legislature Online - 84(R) Text for SB 267. (2015). Texas.gov. https://capitol.texas.gov/billlookup/Text.aspx?LegSess=84R&Bill=SB267

Texas Legislature Online - 84(R) Text for HB 2473. (2015). Texas.gov. https://capitol.texas.gov/billlookup/Text.aspx?LegSess=84R&Bill=HB2473

The Cape Cod Coliseum: All You Need To Know. (2024). CapeCod.com. https://www.capecod.com/lifestyle/the-cape-cod-coliseum-all-you-need-to-know/

The Honorable Brooke L. Rollins. (2024). *Americafirstpolicy.com*. https://americafirstpolicy.com/team/brookerollins

The Honorable Lee Zeldin. (2025). Americafirstpolicy.com. https://www.americafirstpolicy.com/team/the-honorable-lee-zeldin

The Mission and Structure of the Office of Management and Budget. (2017). The White House. https://obamawhitehouse.archives.gov/omb/organization_mission/

Thiel, P. (2009, April 13). *The Education of a Libertarian*. Cato Unbound. https://www.cato-unbound.org/2009/04/13/peter-thiel-education-libertarian/

Tikkanen, A. (2025). *Linda McMahon | Secretary of Education, Confirmation, WWE, & Facts*. Encyclopedia Britannica. https://www.britannica.com/biography/Linda-McMahon

Tims, D. (2016). *Survey: Oregon GOP candidates split on supporting Trump*. Oregonlive. https://www.oregonlive.com/politics/2016/09/survey_oregon_gop_candidates_s.html

The Three Arrows of "Abenomics." (2017). *Prime Minister's Office of Japan*. https://japan.kantei.go.jp/letters/message/abenomics/TheThreeArrowsOfAbenomics_EN.pdf

Tisby, J. (2023). *Congratulations, America. You Have a White Christian Nationalist for Speaker of the House*. Substack.com; Footnotes by Jemar Tisby. https://jemartisby.substack.com/p/congratulations-america-you-have

Tomasky, M. (2024). *Why Does No One Understand the Real Reason Trump Won?* The New Republic. https://newrepublic.com/post/188197/trump-media-information-landscape-fox

Trump, M. L. (2020). *Too Much and Never Enough: How My Family Created the World's Most Dangerous Man*. Simon Schuster.

Trump Transition Update Trump Picks Susie Wiles as Chief of Staff Career Highlights. (2024). https://bgrdc.com/wp-content/uploads/2024/11/Trump-Transition-Update-Susie-Wiles-110824-1.pdf

Tupper, S. (2024). $42,000 lawsuit settlement adds to costs of Noem-ordered border deployments • South Dakota Searchlight. South Dakota Searchlight. https://southdakotasearchlight.com/briefs/42000-lawsuit-settlement-adds-to-costs-of-noem-ordered-border-deployments/

TWS Blog - Military Campaign Stories. (2025). *TWS Blog*. https://blog.togetherweserved.com/maj-pete-hegseth-u-s-army-national-guard-2003-2006-2010-2014-2019-2021/

UN office calls on US to stop separating families at border. (2018). Washington Post; The Washington Post. https://web.archive.org/web/20180614165159/https://www.washingtonpost.com/world/the_americas/un-calls-on-us-to-halt-separations-of-migrant-families/2018/06/05/3fca8a12-68a7-11e8-a335-c4503d041eaf_story.html?utm_term=.3cc69081fb8e

USA gov. (2024). *Branches of the U.S. government*. Usa.gov; USAGov. https://www.usa.gov/branches-of-government

USAspending.gov. (2025). *Usaspending.gov*. https://www.usaspending.gov/agency/small-business-administration?fy=2025

U.S. Department of Health and Human Services. (2024). *About HHS*. HHS.gov. https://www.hhs.gov/about/index.html

U.S. Department of Justice. (2022). *Department of Justice | Federal Bureau of Investigation | United States Department of Justice*. Www.justice.gov. https://www.justice.gov/doj/federal-bureau-investigation

U.S. Department of Veterans Affairs FY 2025 Budget Submission: *Budget in Brief*. (2024). https://department.va.gov/wp-content/uploads/2024/03/fy-2025-va-budget-in-brief.pdf

US EPA. (2019). *EPA's Budget and Spending | US EPA*. US EPA. https://www.epa.gov/planandbudget/budget

USGCRP. (2017). Climate Science Special Report. *Globalchange.gov*, *1*(NCA4), 1–470. https://science2017.globalchange.gov/

U.S. Senate Confirms Jamieson Greer as United States Trade Representative. (2025). United States Trade Representative. https://ustr.gov/about-us/policy-offices/press-office/press-releases/2025/february/us-senate-confirms-jamieson-greer-united-states-trade-representative

Van Zuylen-Wood, S. (2022). *The radicalization of J.D. Vance*. Washington Post. https://www.washingtonpost.com/magazine/2022/01/04/jd-vance-hillbilly-elegy-radicalization/

Voght, K. (2025). *In Karoline Leavitt's world, Trump's word is enough*. The Washington Post. https://www.washingtonpost.com/style/power/2025/03/24/karoline-leavitt-trump-press-secretary/

Vought, Mary Grace Vs Vought, Russell Thurlow | Trellis. (2023). Trellis.Law; Trellis. https://web.archive.org/web/20250211200041/https://trellis.law/case/51013/cl23003105-00/vought-mary-grace-vs-vought-russell-thurlow

Walsh, S. (2025). *How much of the VA's budget savings will go to patient care? Collins says it's "up to the President."* The American Homefront Project; AM HOMEFRONT. https://americanhomefront.wunc.org/news/2025-04-17/how-much-of-the-vas-budget-savings-will-go-to-patient-care-collins-says-its-up-to-the-president

Ward, I. (2024). *55 Things to Know About JD Vance, Trump's VP Pick*. POLITICO; Politico. https://www.politico.com/news/magazine/2024/07/15/jd-vance-55-things-trump-vp-00167882

Waring lll, C. W. (2025). *Digging into President Trump's choice for Treasury: Why South Carolinian Scott Bessent is a wise choice*. Charleston Mercury. https://www.charlestonmercury.com/single-post/digging-into-president-trump-s-choice-for-treasurywhy-south-carolinian-scott-bessent-is-a-wise-choic

Waterhouse, B. (2017). *Donald Trump: Life before the presidency*. Miller Center. https://millercenter.org/president/trump/life-presidency

What led to Mike Waltz's ouster as Trump's national security adviser? (2025). Al Jazeera. https://www.aljazeera.com/news/2025/5/4/what-led-to-mike-waltzs-ouster-as-trumps-national-security-adviser

Wiatrak, S. (2024). *How Kristi Noem's team prepared to defend a $1 million donation to send SD troops to the border - CREW | Citizens for Responsibility and Ethics in Washington*. CREW | Citizens for Responsibility and Ethics in Washington. https://www.citizensforethics.org/reports-investigations/crew-investigations/how-kristi-noems-team-prepared-to-defend-a-1-million-donation-to-send-sd-troops-to-the-border/

Wilhelm Jr, J. (2009). *New business born of Boselli and Wiles partnership*. Jax Daily Record. https://www.jaxdailyrecord.com/news/2009/oct/02/new-business-born-boselli-and-wiles-partnership/

Wilson, J. (2024). *Trump Pentagon pick attacks UN and Nato and urges US to ignore Geneva conventions*. The Guardian; The Guardian. https://www.theguardian.com/us-news/2024/nov/25/pete-hegseth-book-attacks-nato-alliances

Wolf, J. D. (2025). *Pete Hegseth: "I Got Dumber" at Harvard*. MeidasTouch News. https://meidasnews.com/news/pete-hegseth-i-got-dumber-at-harvard

Yang, Y. T. (2024). The perils of RFK Junior's anti-vaccine leadership for public health. *The Lancet*, *405*(10473). https://doi.org/10.1016/s0140-6736(24)02603-5

Yilek, C., & Watson, K. (2025). *Top Trump officials included The Atlantic editor in group chat about plans to bomb Yemen*. Cbsnews.com; CBS News. https://www.cbsnews.com/news/jeffrey-goldberg-the-atlantic-trump-officials-group-chat-signal/

Ziv, S. (2025). *Who would be entitled to a Trump DOGE dividend check?* Forbes Australia. https://www.forbes.com.au/news/world-news/who-would-be-entitled-to-a-trump-doge-dividend-check/

www.ingramcontent.com/pod-product-compliance
Lightning Source LLC
Chambersburg PA
CBHW060351080526
44583CB00012B/271